D1824991

TOLEDO

"Toledo's Enterprises" by Mary Flury Collins

Windsor Publications, Inc.
Chatsworth, California

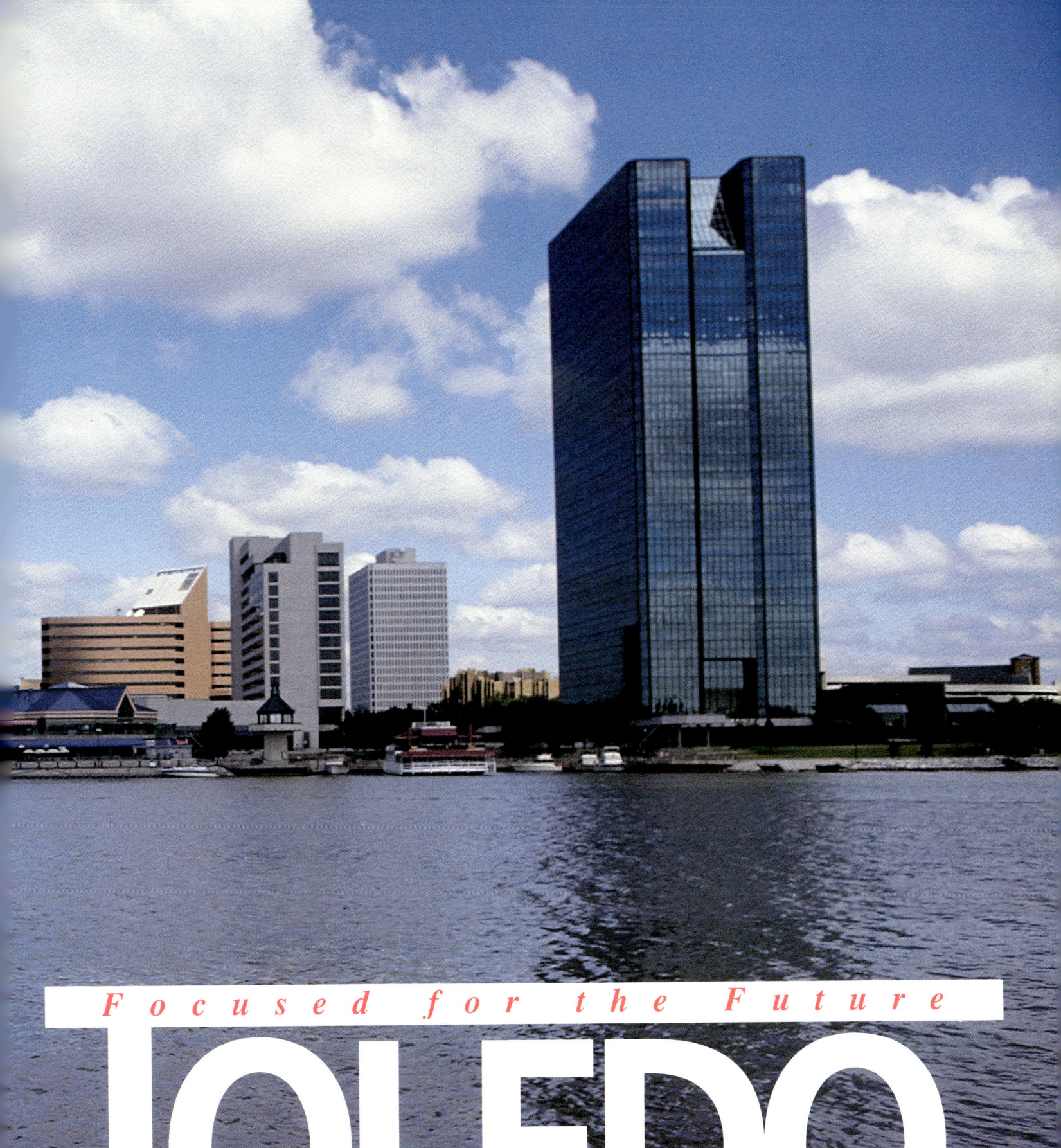

Focused for the Future

TOLEDO

A Contemporary Portrait by Mel Barger

Windsor Publications, Inc.—Book Division
Managing Editor: Karen Story
Design Director: Alexander D'Anca
Photo Director: Susan L. Wells
Executive Editor: Pamela Schroeder

Staff for *Toledo: Focused for the Future*
Manuscript Editor: Susan M. Pahle
Photo Editor: Robin L. Sterling
Production Editor, Text: Michael Nalick
Proofreader: Michael Moore
Editor, Corporate Profiles: Jeffrey Reeves
Production Editor, Corporate Profiles: Justin Scupine
Customer Service Manager: Phyllis Feldman-Schroeder
Editorial Assistants: Elizabeth Anderson, Dominique Jones, Kim Kievman, Michael Nugwynne, Kathy B. Peyser, Theresa J. Solis
Publisher's Representative, Corporate Profiles: R. Zapone, S. Kamman, and R. Lahn
Designer: Alex D'Anca
Layout Artist: Michael Burg

Windsor Publications, Inc.
Elliot Martin, Chairman of the Board
James L. Fish III, Chief Operating Officer
Mac Buhler, Vice President/Acquisitions

Published 1991
Printed in the United States of America
First Edition

Library of Congress Cataloging-in-Publication Data
Barger, Melvin D. Toledo : focused for the future : a contemporary portrait/by Mel Barger
p. 144 cm. 23 x 31
Includes bibliographical references and index.
ISBN: 0-89781-366-9
1. Toledo (Ohio)—Economic conditions. 2. Toledo (Ohio)—Economic conditions—Pictorial works. 3. Toledo (Ohio)—Social conditions. 4. Toledo (Ohio)—Social conditions—Pictorial works. I. Title.
HC108.T6B37 1990 90-44692
977.1'13043--dc20 CIP

FRONTISPIECE: Toledo's dynamic skyline rises along the banks of the flowing Maumee River. Photo by Brad Crooks

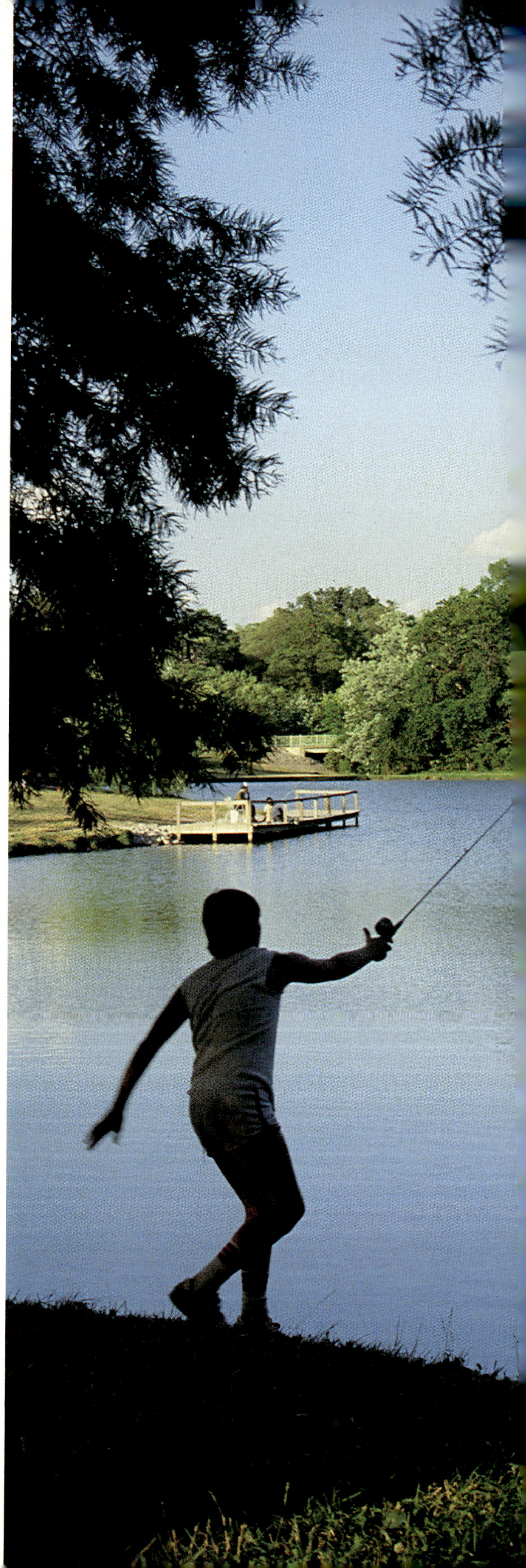

RIGHT: Walden Pond in Ottawa Park is a source of rest and relaxation in the heart of the city and is host to the fun-filled Kid's Fishing Rodeo each year. Photo by Sue Keyser

Contents

PART ONE
Focused for the Future

Chronology 10

CHAPTER ONE
A City of Confidence 12

With its hardworking people, its strong transportation network, and its established economic base, Toledo is re-emerging as a good place to do business.

CHAPTER TWO
The Glass City 26

Toledo built its economic base in the late nineteenth century with the glass industry. Since then, the glass industry as gone through many changes, and Toledo has diversified its industries.

CHAPTER THREE
On the Move 42

Toledo can easily provide sea, air, or land transportation given its proximity to Lake Erie, its modern airport, and the major highways that crisscross the area.

CHAPTER FOUR
Relaxing and Learning in Toledo 52

From the Mud Hens to Maumee State Park to various professional and amateur performing groups to the Toledo Museum of Art, Toledo has plenty of recreational activities to offer its residents and visitors. This city also offers a high quality of education, beginning with kindergarten classes and extending through college and vocational courses.

CHAPTER FIVE
Toledo Reflections 70

As indicated by the flags at International Park on the Maumee River, many different ethnic groups have survived and thrived in Toledo. Residents and visitors alike can enjoy Hungarian hotdogs or participate in kitka dances or visit a German festival

PART TWO
Toledo's Enterprises

CHAPTER SIX
Networks 86

Toledo's role as a modern, thriving metropolitan center is made possible by its network of communication and energy providers.
Columbia Gas of Ohio, 88; WTVG-TV, 89

CHAPTER SEVEN

Business and Professions 90

Toledo's professional community brings a wealth of ability and insight to the area.

Shumaker, Loop & Kendrick, 92; Watkins, Bates, Carey & McHugh, 94; Fuller & Henry, 95; Software Alternatives, Inc., 96; Spengler, Nathanson, Heyman, McCarthy & Durfee, 98; NFO Research, Inc., 100; The Schroeder Company, 102

CHAPTER EIGHT

Quality of Life 104

Medical, educational, and service institutions contribute to the quality of life of Toledo residents.

The University of Toledo, 106; Hospital Council of Northwest Ohio, 108; Envirosafe Services, Inc., 112; Consolidated Environmental Services, Inc. , 113

CHAPTER NINE

Marketplace 114

Toledo's retail establishments and accommodations are enjoyed by residents and visitors.

The Toledo Marriott, 116; Seaway Food Town, 118; Toledo Hilton, 120

CHAPTER TEN

Manufacturing 122

Producing and distributing goods for individuals and industry, manufacturing firms provide employment for Toledo-area residents.

Dana Corporation, 124; Owens-Corning Fiberglas, 126; Hydra-matic Division, 127; Glasstech, Inc., 128; Libbey-Owens-Ford Co., 130; The Kroger Company, 132; TL Industries, Inc., 134; Sun Oil Company, 135

Selected Reading List 139

Directory of Corporate Sponsors 140

Index 141

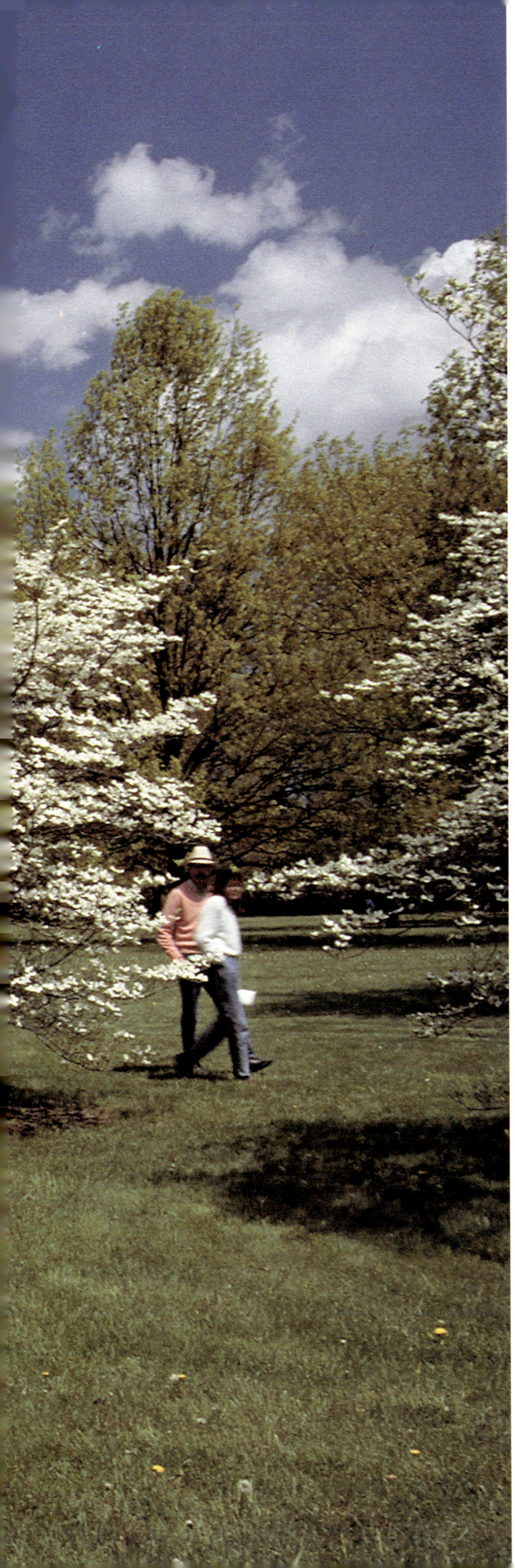

PART ONE

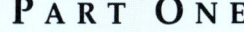

Focused for the Future

Under development since 1966, the R.A. Stranahan Arboretum of the University of Toledo is a living laboratory for many outdoor studies, including botany, biology, and ecology. Photo by Haz Keyser

Chronology
1780-1960

1787 The Northwest Territory Ordinance establishes government in the territory that would later become Ohio, Michigan, Indiana, Illinois, and Wisconsin.

1790 Gabriel Godfrey and John Baptiste Beaugrande, French traders, build a permanent settlement along the Maumee River. Later, this settlement becomes Maumee.

1803 The Ohio state constitution is written, setting the stage for the Toledo War. The war is a dispute between Michigan and Ohio over a strip of land between the two states—a small strip that includes much of present-day Toledo.

1835 (February) Michigan passes a law that prevents Ohio from extending jurisdiction over the disputed strip. This was important because Ohio was trying to complete their part of a canal that extended from the Ohio River to Lake Erie.

The Toledo War consisted mostly of verbal attacks and litigation. Nevertheless, two casualties were reported. A Michigan deputy sheriff was stabbed by a Toledoan who was being arrested for trespassing in the disputed strip. The other casualty was a mule that was shot by a jittery Michigan militiaman. He thought the mule was a Toledo resident.

1835 (September) Ohio claims Toledo and creates Lucas County, with Toledo as the county seat. Legislation required that a common court proceeding be held in the new county. On the day before the proceeding was scheduled, Ohio governor Robert Lucas led Ohio militia into the disputed area, about 12 miles south of Toledo. Meanwhile, Michigan militia were determined to prevent the court from convening. Lucas cleverly led 30 men to Toledo in the middle of the night to carry out the court proceedings. At 3 A.M., the court appointed Lucas County's first commissioners and a clerk. Lucas and his men then hastily retreated to the Ohio border just ahead of the Michigan militia. During the ride home, however, the newly appointed clerk lost his hat in which he had stored the official minutes of the meeting. Without the minutes, the court meeting was not legal. Early in the morning, the hat and the minutes were luckily found.

1836 Michigan is granted statehood. The U.S. Congress awarded 9,000 square miles (the Upper Peninsula) to Michigan since it lost 450 square miles to Ohio in the Toledo War.

1837 The city of Toledo is chartered. The town was originally formed by the merger of two villages—Port Lawrence and Vistula.

1843 The canal opens and the first boat arrives from Indiana. Toledo was already an important lake port, but the canal increased the shipping of goods to and from the growing interior. Canal boatmen dubbed the city Frog Town. The source of the nickname was Mud Creek, a local swamp. It was drained in the 1870s and 1880s, then graded so that streets could be built.

1850 Toledo calls itself the Corn City because of the large quantities of corn shipped through its canal, railroad, and port.

1860 German and Irish immigrants come to Toledo ready to supply labor for Toledo's growing industries. Polish immigrants arrived in the 1870s.

1888 Toledo's population is 50,000, a significant increase from its 1850 population of 20,000. Also during the 1880s, natural gas is discovered in Findlay, Ohio, about 40 miles from Toledo. This find helps spur development of Toledo's glass industries.

1888 Edward Drummond Libbey moves his New England Glass Company to Toledo, where it is renamed the Libbey Glass Company. Libbey was sooned joined in business by Michael J. Owens, who developed machines for the mass production of light bulbs and bottles. The two glass pioneers also formed the Libbey-Owens Sheet Glass Company in 1917.

1890 Peter Gendron begins making bicycles in his wire wheel factory. In the next few years, Toledo becomes home to more than a dozen bicycle-manufacturing companies during a short-lived bicycle boom that helped lay the groundwork for the infant automobile industry.

1898 Edward Ford purchases a site across the Maumee River from Toledo and establishes the town of Rossford as the home of his new Edward Ford Plate Glass Company. Opened in 1899, the plant becomes the nation's leading producer of quality plate glass and, in 1930, is merged with Libbey-Owens Sheet Glass to form Libbey-Owens-Ford Glass Company.

1900 Dr. Allen DeVilbiss and his son Thomas open the DeVilbiss Company. The company manufactured an atomizer, which Dr. DeVilbiss had invented so that medication could be sprayed into the nose. By 1909, the company used the atomizing technology to develop and manufacture paint-spraying equipment. Another of DeVilbiss' sons, Allen, invented a springless, automatic computing scale. The scale was unique in its day because it displayed the weight and cost of the object being sold. In 190l, DeVilbiss sold the patent for his scale to the Toledo Scale and Cash Register Company. By 1910, the Toledo Scale Company had sold more than 75,000 scales.

1907 The Pope Motor Car Company is formed by the merger of the Lozier Manufacturing Company and the A.A. Pope American Bicycle Company. Both of these companies originally built bicycles and later built steam-powered vehicles. Today the Toledo Chrysler Jeep plant is

Constructed in 1813 under the supervision of General William Henry Harrison, Fort Meigs is considered to be the largest walled fortification in North America and stands as a reminder of Toledo's colorful past. Photo by Haz Keyser

housed on the site of the Pope Motor Company, one of the oldest automobile factories in the world.

1941 Two car companies submit proposals to the U.S. Government at the beginning of World War II to build a general purpose, or G.P., vehicle for the army. The Willys-Overland Company wins the bid and produces more than 300,000 Jeeps between 1941 and 1945. Dwight Eisenhower called the vehicle the "workhorse" of the war. Today the Jeep survives as an all-purpose, four-wheel-drive vehicle.

1954 The Toledo Express Airport opens.

1959 The St. Lawrence Seaway opens, making Toledo and other Great Lakes ports international ports of call.

CHAPTER ONE

A City of Confidence

T oledo is facing the 1990s with renewed confidence and strategic plans for future stability. It's re-emerging as a great place to do business, building on community strengths the city has always possessed. Edward J. Schulte, deputy director of economic development for the Toledo-Lucas County Port Authority explains, "You have to remember that the same things that make Toledo a nice place to live also make it a good place to do business." Some of the assets he notes include Toledo's location, its easy access to transportation facilities, the community's outstanding educational facilities, and a skilled, well-educated work force, as well as easy access to important markets and a ready supply of the services most businesses need.

Toledo is a city that found its strong economic base during the swift industrial expansion of the late nineteenth century and the growth of the automobile age. Its early expansion was so impressive that a

Once the king of the Great Lakes shipping freighters when first launched in 1911, the stately *Willis B. Boyer* provides an entertaining and educational glimpse into the past. This faithful restoration is open to the public from May until September and is located along the banks of the Maumee River at International Park. Photo by Brad Crooks

ABOVE: The shimmering lights of downtown Toledo reflect off the waters of the Maumee River as evening falls over the city. Photo by Sue Keyser

RIGHT: According to J. Michael Porter, president of the Toledo Area Chamber of Commerce, Toledo has ". . . the benefits of large-city amenities without the problems associated with big-city life." Photo by Sue Keyser

FACING PAGE: Boating is a favorite Toledo pastime and the city offers a host of docking facilities for thousands of area boats. Photo by Brad Crooks

writer in 1912 depicted Toledo as a city that "could not help itself—it had to be an industrial center, because of its very location . . . It is the natural meeting place of iron ore from the north and coal from the south." He went on to describe Toledo's great diversified industries: plate and cut glass, automobiles, computing scales, engines, boats and a large assortment of auto parts.

Today Toledo is still an industrial center, receiving iron ore from the north and coal from the south. And Toledo's location is still important to its future. In the opinion of Hank Harvey, transportation writer for *The Blade* (Toledo's daily newspaper), Toledo has the best location of any port city on the Great Lakes. "Our diversity makes Toledo different from other Great Lakes ports such as Duluth, Cleveland, and Detroit," Harvey says. "We receive and ship general

cargo along with grain, coal, and iron ore, while other Great Lakes ports are heavily weighted to only one or two of these commodities. Because of this diversity, we'll always be in business."

Additionally, Toledo is a center for railroad and truck transportation and it adjoins two great interstate highways: I-75 spans the eastern United States north and south, and I-80 is a great east and west artery. There's also the busy Toledo Express Airport, a mere 20 minutes or so from downtown Toledo.

Even in 1912, though depicted as a city that succeeded largely because of its location, Toledo's real growth came from the purposeful efforts of its energetic, hardworking people. They brought their confidence and skills to the city and helped it grow. Today a new generation of people are contributing the same kind of confidence to the city's resurgence in the 1990s. Moreover, they're well-trained, well-educated people who are very much in tune with the needs of the 1990s and the era stretching out beyond the year 2000.

Nobody discounts the importance of location, however, and Toledo has always had an advantage since it's located at the very western tip of Lake Erie. By expressway travel, Toledo is two hours west of Cleveland and an hour south of Detroit. It's also about three hours north of Columbus, the Ohio state capital, and about four hours east of Chicago.

Toledo's elevation is 585 feet, only 15 feet higher than Lake Erie. With the exception of a few gentle hills laced with creek floodplains and ravines, most of the city and surrounding area have an entirely flat landscape. Toledo owes this topographical feature to the great glaciers that once covered the region and also gave it a covering of rich topsoil. Those same glaciers left the moraines that formed Michigan's beautiful Irish Hills and also helped shape the lovely lakelands to the north, which are favorite vacation spots for Toledo residents.

Some of Toledo's eastern and northern perimeters are defined by water: Lake Erie, Maumee Bay, and the Maumee River. The Maumee River flows northeast through downtown Toledo, while the lake and bay are several miles to the north and east of the main part of the city. Most of the western Lake Erie shore is easily accessible to Toledo, making the area one of the world's great centers for fishing and boating. Western Lake Erie, in fact, is famous for year-round fishing for walleye and perch.

On its western, northern, southern, and some eastern boundaries, Toledo is surrounded by flat, rich farmland and pleasant villages. On its northern boundary, Toledo also abuts Michigan, whose nearby communities of Lambertville and Temperance are Toledo suburbs. It is important locally that the city adjoins Michigan's southern border and occupies most of an area that Michigan sought to claim back in 1830. (This proximity to Michigan may explain why Toledoans appear to be almost equally divided in their loyalties when the intense gridiron rivalry between the University of Michigan and Ohio State University is played out every November.)

Thanks to those topsoil deposits from the glacial ages, the greater Toledo area is a highly productive region for fruits, grain crops, tomatoes, and other vegetables. In season, some of the towns near Toledo are rich with the cooking aromas of local canneries processing the region's tomato production.

Toledo is the kind of city that has both the cosmopolitan and the rural within a few minutes of each other. Because of a system of excellent country roads,

15

people who work in or near the city can also choose to live in small towns beyond the immediate suburbs of Toledo.

Toledo itself is a good mixture of old and new neighborhoods with a dozen expanding suburbs on its perimeter and one very upscale community, Ottawa Hills, as an enclave surrounded by the city. Some of the older sections of the city show signs of urban decay, but this has been partly offset by housing programs and other efforts to revitalize the city. Two of the most successful efforts have been the campaigns to stabilize Toledo's downtown and a nearby residential community, the Old West End.

Downtown Toledo, once the hub of the city's retail business, has been the focus of much discussion and renewal effort during the past 20 years. It is no longer a major retail center; this has shifted to several large malls and smaller shopping centers scattered strategically throughout the metropolitan area. What Toledo now seeks in its downtown section is stability and enhancement for the new buildings and facilities that have been constructed in the past 12 years. At the same time, it wants to preserve the older institutions that have been vital to the city's progress.

Two adjoining villages, Port Lawrence and Vistula, became the downtown when the city was formed in 1837. Like most cities that grew up on rivers, Toledo's downtown streets are at angles to many other streets in the areas that were added to the city later on. There is some system, however, to the naming of the downtown streets. Except for Summit and St. Clair streets, the downtown streets paralleling the Maumee River are named for the Great Lakes: Superior, Huron, Erie, Ontario, and Michigan. The streets at right angles to the river are named for American presidents.

One of these, Monroe Street, is a major Toledo thoroughfare that continues in a northwest direction for about 10 miles through much of Toledo into Sylvania before heading up towards Michigan's scenic Irish Hills as U.S. Route 223. A *Blade* reporter, Homer Brickey, walked the entire 10 miles of Monroe Street in 1973 and again in 1983 just to produce slice-of-life stories about Saturday nights in Toledo.

The 1973 story was prompted by John Denver's popular song, *Saturday Night in Toledo, Ohio*, written by Randy Sparks. Considered a put-down by some Toledoans, it suggested that a single Saturday night in

on at One Government Center and the adjoining public buildings. A continuing issue is that of political and economic cooperation between the city and the suburbs, as well as the type of government that's best for the city. Since 1934 Toledo has had a city-manager type of government, with the mayor serving in a policy-making capacity and as a council member. But there have been recent moves to restore the "strong mayor" type of system, which would again place the mayor directly in charge of administration and other key functions.

Also in the downtown is the Lucas County Courthouse, which occupies a one-block square

Toledo was so boring that it seemed like two weeks! But the song turned out to be positive for the city when Denver himself performed before sellout audiences in Toledo at the University of Toledo's Centennial Hall. And it was Denver's *Saturday Night in Toledo* that brought the crowd to its feet!

Monroe Street has changed dramatically in the past 20 years and reflects along its entire length a good cross-section of the outlying commercial and residential growth that characterizes Toledo.

The other U.S. presidents who are honored by Toledo's downtown street names include Washington, Jefferson, Madison, Adams, and Jackson. With the city's downtown transformations of the past 10 years, Jackson Street became a beautifully landscaped boulevard extending outward from a corner of One SeaGate, on the river.

One Government Center, a 22-story building that houses city, county, and state offices, is also located downtown. Often called the City/County Building, it adjoins four other governmental buildings clustered in several large city blocks.

The building may achieve lasting recognition as a creation of the late Minoru Yamasaki, the chief designer of New York's World Trade Center complex. Known for the delicate patterns of his building exteriors, Yamasaki gave the effect of a "punched-window" design to the outside of One Government Center. Occupying a plaza on Jackson Street, the new government building serves both a functional purpose and also symbolizes Toledo's continuing revitalization.

Toledoans pay a lot of attention to what's going

ABOVE: Blending with Toledo's modern office structures, the venerable Lucas County Courthouse is a tribute to the city's historic past. Dedicated in 1897, the courthouse is guarded by a statue of President William McKinley. Photo by Ken Osburn/ Third Coast Stock Source

FACING PAGE: The successful rejuvenation of downtown Toledo is evident in the city's striking skyline. Photo by Herral Long

TOP LEFT: Designed by the late Minoru Yamasaki, One Government Center houses city, county, and state offices and is representative of Toledo's continuing revitalization. Photo by Barbara Durham

LEFT: The magnificent Rosary Cathedral is a prominent Old West End institution and now serves as the main worship center of the Toledo Catholic diocese. Photo by Jeanne Conte

FACING PAGE: A dusting of snow turns the Old West End into a winter wonderland. Photo by Sue Keyser

guide, published by Lawrence Publications, Inc., noted, the homes in the Old West End neighborhoods "represent a vanished era of crystal chandeliers, wood paneling, servants and carriage houses." In this bygone era, the residents of the Old West End would have included glass pioneers Edward Drummond Libbey and Michael J. Owens. And two prominent institutions still important to these glass pioneers and to Toledo are located in the Old West End: The Toledo Museum of Art, largely the creation of Libbey, and Rosary Cathedral, the headquarters of the Toledo Catholic diocese, to which Owens belonged.

Though the Old West End is no longer the neighborhood of the wealthy, it's a source of pride in Toledo because people who lived there banded together in an improvement association and halted the decay that obviously began setting in when the move to the suburbs began in the 1950s. While many of the old homes are now headquarters for service and cultural organizations, the Old West End is considered by many to be a nice place to live. It's considered chic among young, well-educated people to live in the area, and many of the old mansions are now attractive apartment houses. Old West Enders seem to enjoy the arts and crafts, modern entertainment, and running events; they even have their own yearly festival with a 10K race.

Farther north the city becomes West Toledo and, nearer Lake Erie, an area loosely described as North Toledo. Both parts of the city have neighborhoods of older, well-kempt homes and newer sections of medium-priced bungalows and ranch houses built in

diagonally across Jackson Street from One Government Center. The old domed courthouse was dedicated in 1897, the first year of the McKinley Administration and has remained one of the great achievements of Toledo's past. Guarding the courthouse is a statue of President McKinley, looking out across Adams Street towards the southwest. At that same Adams Street entrance, the terrazzo courthouse floor has an inlaid frog design. According to Toledo historian Tana Mosier Porter, this reminds visitors that the site was once a swamp. There are still efforts in Toledo to revive this old image of the city as Frogtown, but the real frogs left the city with the disappearance of the swamp.

Not in the downtown area, but adjoining it, is the Old West End—a section with graceful, elegant old homes built by Toledo's affluent elite during the growth years of the late nineteenth and early twentieth centuries. As the Toledo Metropolitan City-

the post-World War II era. Both West Toledo and North Toledo have factory areas, including small manufacturing plants and warehouse sections often adjoining residential neighborhoods. Except for a few areas of decay, however, much of Toledo's residential area is considered highly stable.

This is also true of East Toledo, an older part of the city located across the Maumee River from downtown Toledo. East Toledo has many sections of row-type houses built on narrow lots in the early years of the century, and it has a number of factories and processing facilities.

Toledoans also refer to "South" Toledo, which may seem more west to many visitors and newcomers. South Toledo has many older neighborhoods closer to the downtown area, with many residential areas becoming generally newer and more upscale further north and west of downtown Toledo. However, some of Toledo's finest older residential sections are on River Road, which parallels the Maumee River southeast into the city of Maumee.

For location reference points Toledoans often use either the names of suburbs in general areas or the large shopping malls that have become the city's retail centers. One suburb of particular note, however, is Ottawa Hills, which is partly within Toledo's north-

western boundaries. It's definitely "class" to have even a modest home in Ottawa Hills. Developed after World War I as a "garden suburb," Ottawa Hills was patterned after similar enclaves in Baltimore and Cleveland. Though many of its homes are of medium size, Ottawa Hills also has a number of Toledo's finest estates, still occupied by people who can afford to maintain them. Curving streets and gently sloping hills, unusual for the Toledo area, add to the grandeur of this village.

In recent years Hasty Hills has been developed west of Ottawa Hills. It represents the kind of high-priced development that's been taking place in several large areas in the southwest, west, and northwest suburbs of Toledo. Hasty Hills' streets follow the same curving patterns of a garden community with broad, sweeping lawns and elegant homes built to take advantage of the rolling hills and ravines of the area. At its western edge is Exmoor, a walled community of beautiful, very pricey homes built to minimize yard area while retaining maximum privacy for the individual family.

The suburban areas that surround Toledo have special characteristics and are identified by economic levels, in general. Across the state line to the north, in Michigan, is Bedford Township with the villages of Lambertville and Temperance. It's a great place for people who like an acre or more of land, some with small hills and wooded lots. There are riding stables here, and some families even like to keep a horse.

Sylvania and Sylvania Township, on Toledo's northwest side, are considered middle- to upper-class communities with lots of business and professional people. There are a number of more modest residential areas in Holland and Springfield Township west of Toledo, including some mobile home parks. But it's an area of continuing growth, and the

most recent innovation has been the construction of Springfield Meadows, a huge open mall with more than a hundred outlets clustered in the area.

Maumee and Perrysburg adjoin Toledo on the southwestern side. Maumee is an excellent place to live with homes in many price ranges, while also having some of the area's historic old homes within its borders. It is also the site of Arrowhead Park, an industrial and office development with 9,000 employees who work for various tenant companies, many of them entrepreneurial ventures in new, high-tech-related industries.

Perrysburg rivals Ottawa Hills as a Toledo-area "class" community, though many of the homes within the town are actually rather modest. But it's a place of quiet streets with a beautiful overlook of the Maumee River all along its northern edge. Several of the old estates along the river in the Perrysburg area have been transformed into elegant condominium developments.

Rossford, which connects to Perrysburg, has been a factory town from the beginning and is still the site of a huge Libbey-Owens-Ford plate-glass plant. The nearby towns of Oregon and Northwood also have a number of plants and factories, but this hasn't slowed residential development. Oregon and several villages

FACING PAGE, TOP: Sweeping lawns and elegant homes are characteristic of the affluent Hasty Hills community. Photo by Sue Keyser

FACING PAGE, BOTTOM: From charming ethnic festivals to challenging athletic competitions, Toledo is rich with a host of events and activities for young and old alike. Photo by Haz Keyser

ABOVE: Located northwest of the city, Sylvania is the largest suburban community in Toledo's metropolitan region and offers a fine selection of housing from which to choose a family home. Photo by Sue Keyser

beyond it—Millbury, Elmore, Genoa—view themselves as more than mere suburbs of Toledo. Oregon, in fact, has substantial retail areas and a total population of about 20,000.

There are at least three ways to look at Toledo's population. One is the population count within the city limits. Toledo's official population is estimated to be about 355,000, and this could shrink slightly when the 1990 census is tallied. A second way to compute population is to use the federal Toledo Metropolitan Statistical Area (MSA) estimates. Toledo's MSA total

The Toledo region provides a wealth of boating opportunities, from the high-speed thrill of powerboating to a leisurely afternoon ride along a quiet waterway. Photo by Herral Long

of about 615,000 includes Lucas County (Toledo is the county seat), and two adjoining counties, Wood and Fulton. A third way to view population—one that is important to businesses like broadcasters, wholesale distributors, and retailers—is to focus on the general trade area. According to *Sales & Marketing Management* magazine, this larger area includes the two southeastern Michigan counties, Lenawee and Monroe, which adjoin Toledo, as well as 12 counties in northwest Ohio—a total area population of 1,238,000.

Kent J. Galvin, general manager of the Toledo Area Chamber of Commerce, feels that 600,000, which approximates the MSA count, is the better figure for Toledo-related population. But Schulte points out that MSA figures stop arbitrarily at county lines, while people trade and shop according to convenience, needs, and preferences. There's good reason to believe, however, that a larger part of the better-paying employment for the general trade area is concentrated in Lucas, Wood, and Fulton counties. There are about 285,000 employed in this three-county area, with about one-fourth of the jobs centered in manufacturing. The largest segments of nonmanufacturing employment are in services of various kinds, as well as retail trade and government. Since the early 1970s, there's been anxiety in Toledo about the future of the heavy manufacturing industries—particularly the glass and auto-supplier companies. While there have been major plant-closings and other shutdowns, there's also growing confidence that these job losses are being offset by steady increases in medium-sized companies, which also have excellent prospects for future growth. Manufacturing employment in the Toledo area has admittedly declined since 1975. But total Toledo MSA employment is up substantially for the same time period.

Toledo's strong educational institutions add up to one advantage, which many feel should help the city employment and economic growth in the future. Toledo and the suburban communities are credited with having excellent public and parochial schools,

local school systems. With training grants from the Ohio Industrial Training Program and the availability of qualified schools, more than 120 companies in the area have received assistance in employee training.

In line with the same standards that helped give the Toledo area leadership in education, the community is also known for the development of its cultural institutions: the Toledo Museum of Art, the Toledo Symphony Orchestra, the Toledo Opera Association, several highly acclaimed amateur theater groups, and a professional dinner theater. The Toledo Zoo, recently enlarged, continues to improve its programs for the community.

Toledo is known, too, for its sports. Its leading professional sports team is the Toledo Mud Hens in minor league baseball. The city is also considered to be one of the three or four leading bowling centers in the nation and annually hosts major tournaments. In golf, Toledo's famed Inverness Country Club has hosted several National Open Tournaments since 1920 and has been the host club for the PGA Tournament. Toledo also has been the site of the LPGA Jamie Farr Toledo Open for several years, most recently at Highland Meadows Golf Club.

In addition to fishing and boating on Lake Erie and nearby lakes, Toledo has numerous city and county parks with well-developed facilities. What's bringing the greatest excitement, however, is the 1990 completion of the Maumee Bay State Park a few miles east of the city—the first large-scale state park in Northwest Ohio. Facing Lake Erie, the park has a $20-million lodge with meeting facilities and all the amenities of a resort hotel. It's expected to draw 4 million visitors a year to the Toledo area.

Despite its diversity by neighborhood and other distinctions within the community, Toledo has much solidarity among its citizens on matters that really count. There's much agreement, for example, on the point that Toledo is a nice place to live, whether your home is a small bungalow in West Toledo or a mansion in Ottawa Hills. It's becoming a nicer place to visit, and the city is attracting more conventions as well as touring groups. And Toledo continues to be a great place for business—and should be even better as the 1990s decade wears on.

TOP: The federal Toledo Metropolitan Statistical Area estimates bring the total of Toledo's population to about 615,000—a figure that encompasses the residents of Lucas, Wood, and Fulton counties. Photo by Herral Long

ABOVE: Cross-country skiing has become a popular wintertime activity in Northwest Ohio, and Toledoans enjoy first-rate conditions for this exhilarating sport. Photo by Haz Keyser

including high-school-level training for vocational purposes as well as for college preparation. The six-county area including and surrounding Toledo, has two major state universities, an important medical college that graduates medical personnel as well as doctors, two four-year liberal arts colleges, and three two-year vocational colleges, in addition to excellent

John McHugh:
A Mayor Seeking Community-wide Cooperation

"I want the signs taken down at the city limits," Toledo Mayor John McHugh told a visitor several weeks after taking office. "If we operate in Northwest Ohio, we can't just look at the city of Toledo. We have to look at it as a region."

Though the city boundary signs are likely to stay for the time being, McHugh's comment expressed his deep conviction that the city of Toledo needs to look outside its own perimeter. With its population of about 350,000, Toledo needs to work more closely with the adjoining suburban areas where nearly a quarter of a million people live, he feels. "If we're going to grow, we'll have to cooperate, and this has been a major goal of mine."

McHugh took office on December 1, 1989. Under Toledo's city-manager form of government, mayoral authority is limited to a vote on the city council and control over policy. But McHugh, who captured 71 percent of the vote, also has a strong personal following as well as considerable experience in gov-

ernment. And both the community and Toledo media tend to look to the mayor's office for leadership when important issues arise.

McHugh, a man who makes friends easily, may have the right qualities for his new role, which includes representing the city at public functions and managing considerable liaison with state and federal officials. Upon taking office, he quickly became known as a mayor who would listen to all groups in the community. One of his first actions was to begin meeting with the heads of various Toledo companies in an effort to help the city's economic development and business retention. He also began meeting with suburban leaders, including the new mayor of Oregon, in a campaign to obtain more cooperation on matters of common interest in the region.

As the son of Irish-born parents, McHugh also has a feeling for the city's ethnic diversities, where more than 80 nationalities are represented. He grew up in Toledo and attended Central Cath-

olic High School and the University of Toledo before going into governmental employment. He became Lucas County recorder in 1971 and also served as Lucas County treasurer, later resigning to become chairman of his political party.

It was as party chairman that McHugh first decided to run for the mayor's office. The suggestion came from his wife, Connie, a retired school teacher. Though he squeaked by with only one vote in the party's selection process, his overwhelming victory in the general election virtually constitutes a mandate.

"McHugh favors a return to the "strong mayor" type of government for Toledo but currently calls it a "back-burner" issue. Nor will he really say whether he would run for the post if it is restructured by the voters. In the meantime, however, he's obviously determined to be a strong mayor in pushing his convictions about what's needed for the city's future.

Photo by Herral Long

CHAPTER TWO

The
Glass City

Glass City is still synonymous with Toledo. The leaders of more than 30 organizations and businesses still use the name proudly for identification. There's a Glass City Roofing, for example, along with a Glass City Autosport and a Glass City Gymnastics, and numerous other firms named for Toledo's traditional industry.

But the major companies that made Toledo the nation's glass empire have undergone profound changes since the mid-1970s. Owens-Illinois, the largest, has been restructured. Owens-Corning Fiberglas, after fighting a takeover, also underwent restructuring. Libbey-Owens-Ford, though still bearing its own name and a high degree of independence, was acquired in 1986 by Pilkington, a British glass firm. Manville, the other Toledo-area firm of great prominence in the glass industry, was renamed Manville Sales Corporation following a corporate decision to drop its former name, Johns-Manville.

Known as the heart of the nation's glass industry, Toledo has evolved into a dynamic center of business and industry. One of the city's three major glass companies, Owens-Corning, is developing new and exciting applications for today's fiberglass products. One such useful application is pictured here at this construction site. Photo by Jim Rohman

Restructuring brought staff reductions at Owens-Illinois, Owens-Corning, and Libbey-Owens-Ford. Libbey-Owens-Ford also shut down two glass plants that had operated in East Toledo since the late 1920s.

All three glass companies have maintained a strong grip on their markets and have continued to plan for future progress. Owens-Illinois has diversified into health care, Owens-Corning continues to develop new uses for fiberglass, and Libbey-Owens-Ford is making additional innovations in automotive and architectural glass, its two major markets. Manville Sales Corporation, located southwest of Toledo near the village of Waterville, produces fiberglass for aircraft and other industry. This company has augmented its research and development staff at the local plant; the staff now totals about 800. The Manville Toledo-area employment is twice its level of 12 to 15 years ago, which is unique since many glass-related industries have cut back.

Toledo's role as the Glass Capital has positively encouraged the development of glass-related industries as well. Four of the most prominent are Glasstech, Inc., Tempglass, Inc., Glassline Corporation, and Royal Tool Inc., all highly successful in their markets. Glasstech innovates, designs, and fabricates glass-bending and tempering equipment for the automotive and architectural industries and is also developing equipment for manufacturing photovoltaic cells. Tempglass custom fabricates horizontally tempered glass, insulated glass, laminated glass, and spandrels for the architectural market. Glassline designs and fabricates equipment and diamond tooling for glass manufacturing. Royal Tool designs and builds machines for glass grinding, drilling, polishing, and edging.

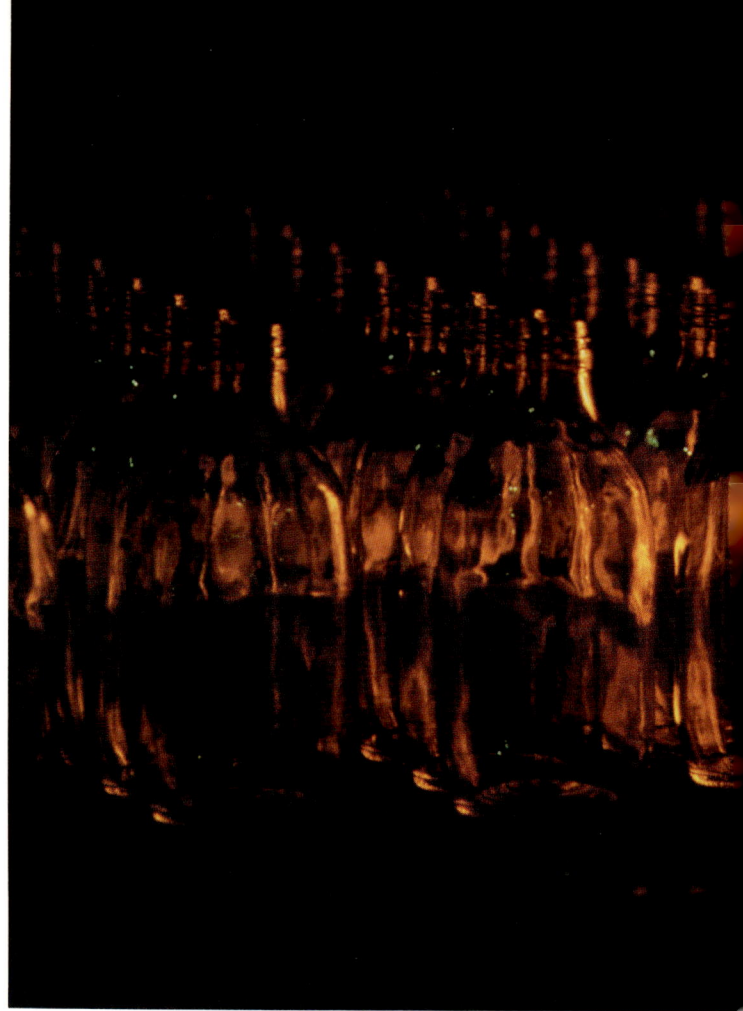

Downtown Toledo, in addition to being world headquarters for Owens-Illinois, is also headquarters for two other major glass companies that helped make Toledo the Glass City. Owens-Corning Fiberglas (OCF) is headquartered in the 30-story Fiberglas Tower, and Libbey-Owens-Ford (LOF) is about four blocks northwest in the 15-story LOF Tower. OCF is the world's leading manufacturer of glass-fiber-related products, while LOF is a major producer of flat glass for the automotive and construction industries as well as specialty markets.

Also based in Toledo's downtown area is the Toledo-Lucas County Port Authority, which has responsibility for seaport and aviation activities in the area and spearheads economic development and business retention and creation. The Toledo *Blade*, the city's daily newspaper, is headquartered in the area, along with WTOL-TV Channel 11, the city's CBS affiliate, and WGTE-TV Channel 30, the public broadcasting station. (WTVG-TV Channel 13, the NBC affiliate, is in a suburban part of South Toledo, as is WNWO-TV Channel 24, the ABC affiliate.) Additional major organizations in the downtown district include Toledo Edison, Bostwick-Braun Co., AP Parts, So-

LEFT: The strength of Toledo's leading glass corporations has encouraged the growth of successful glass-related industries. Photo by Jim Rohman

BELOW: Plate-glass manufacturing for architectural use at Libbey-Owens-Ford employs state-of-the-art facilities and equipment. Photo by Jim Rohman

FACING PAGE: A Libbey-Owens-Ford employee inspects the glass flow inside a furnace with the use of an industrial-strength shield. This safeguard measure protects him from the brilliant light and searing heat of the furnace. Photo by Jim Rohman

ciety Bank, Fifth Third Bank, and SSOE, Inc., a noted architectural and engineering firm.

The other major companies located in Toledo—though not in the downtown district—are Dana Corp.; Doehler-Jarvis; Dura Automatic Hardware; General Mills, Inc.; Sun Refining; BP Oil Co.; Teledyne CAE; Glasstech, Inc.; Champion Spark Plug Co.; Seaway Foodtown, Inc.; The Andersons; and TRINOVA Corp. And all of the Big Three American automobile manufacturers have Toledo-area plants, including the Chrysler Jeep plant near downtown Toledo.

Toledo also has other major industrial companies, including local plants operated by General Motors, Ford, and Chrysler. While manufacturers, refineries, and utilities with employment of more than 200 provide a total of about 37,000 jobs in the Toledo area, local development officials are doubtful that these employers will drive Toledo's future growth and progress. The community is making determined efforts to maintain its current industries and to enhance the business climate to attract new opportunities. The greatest future vitality could come from smaller entrepreneurial organizations and from service companies, many employing highly trained professional and technical personnel.

In the Toledo area, the lead economic development agency is the Toledo-Lucas County Port Authority. Port authority officials, after successful passage of

a tax levy in late 1989, allocated $1.1 million to economic development. One goal of the program, according to Clarence D. Pawlicki, economic development director, is to work closely with the Toledo area's 1,000 manufacturing firms to encourage them to remain in the community. Another function of the agency is to contact firms throughout the world to encourage them to build plants in Toledo.

One of the port authority's most successful programs is the Northwest Ohio Bond Fund, which issues tax-exempt industrial revenue bonds to small- and medium-sized manufacturing firms that are

cess to make photovoltaic cells that directly convert sunlight into electricity.

As for the future of Toledo manufacturing, Edward J. Schulte, the port authority's deputy director of economic development, is counting on substantial future growth in plastics operations, small high-tech growth firms, and auto-related companies. It's still signficant that more than 40 types of automobile components are manufactured in Toledo, including such big-ticket items as transmissions and suspension systems.

The general field of plastics has exciting opportunities for Toledo. "Toledo is fast becoming the nation's plastics capital," Schulte has noted. He explains that the city is located within 500 miles of 50 percent of the plastics market and is also close to North American industrial markets and most of the automotive market. A growing number of Toledo companies are engaged in state-of-the-art plastics production. "We have what plastics manufacturers need," Schulte points out. "We have local refineries as convenient sources for the specialty resins and chemicals essential to plastics production. There are more than 100 tool-and-die companies located in the Toledo area to provide the support services needed by the plastics firms. Many of them have CAD/CAM facilities and are staffed with people who understand the plastics business."

Schulte also believes plastics growth in Toledo is getting a substantial boost from the University of Toledo, which has the UT Polymer Institute as a resource for research and education and also offers a full array of engineering and engineering technologies majors in polymeric materials studies and sciences. The UT Community Technical College and Owens Technical College both offer training in plastics-related technologies, and further educational opportunities and research assistance are available at Bowling Green State University and the University of Michigan, both within an hour's drive of Toledo.

Schulte believes that the Toledo area's excellent educational and research facilities also will help drive growth in small high-tech businesses, the second important area the community has targeted. One new

ABOVE: An outstanding achievement of modern architecture, the 30-story Fiberglas Tower houses the headquarters of Owens-Corning Fiberglas. Photo by Ken Osburn/ Third Coast Stock Source

FACING PAGE: In addition to its stable glass industry, Toledo is rapidly becoming a major plastics manufacturer. These 55-gallon storage drums, produced by Owens-Illinois, are rapidly replacing the steel containers of yesterday. Photo by Jim Rohman

creditworthy, but have not been able to attract investors in the national capital market. Some of the local projects funded under this plan include an $18-million grain terminal (for Cargill), new taconite docks worth more than $30 million, and an engineering office building for Teledyne CAE. The program also assisted Solar Cells, Inc., a new high-tech firm, which utilizes a revolutionary manufacturing pro-

industry profile in the belief that future strength in this field is still possible. This runs strongly counter to the pessimism of the early 1980s, when automotive suppliers were retrenching, diversifying, or simply getting out of the business. With automotive supply and assembly plants opening in low-wage countries throughout the world, the future appeared bleak for the larger industrial cities of North America.

What brightened this outlook? For one thing, the early 1980s analysts were studying the industry during one of its severely recessed periods. They failed to take into account the ability of U.S. auto manufacturers to restructure and come back with more competitive models. The recovery got a boost, too, from a good deal of cost-cutting initiated by suppliers. LOF, for example, developed encapsulated windows that enable auto manufacturers to eliminate certain high-cost assembly steps.

research resource for this type of development is the Edison Industrial Systems Center, a public/private consortium established in 1987 under Ohio's Thomas Edison Program to stimulate technological innovation and enterprise in the state. Supported by both state and private funding, the center provides a number of computer-driven services necessary for high-tech development, particularly in modeling and simulations.

The center's resources enable member companies and organizations to avail themselves of state-of-the-art technological information and databases at significant savings in time and costs. At the same time, there is a pooling of information and experience as a result of the consortium idea, which is being adopted in a number of U.S. high-tech industries to meet fierce global competition. Major organizations who are cooperating in the center's work include Digital Equipment Corporation and Hewlett-Packard Corporation, as well as the University of Toledo, Bowling Green State University, and the Medical College of Ohio.

In a similar way, the Thin Film Institute at the University of Toledo seeks to develop new products utilizing coatings of film on glass. Heading the institute is Dr. Alvin Compaan, a physicist. The institute is currently working with Solar Cells and Glasstech on the development of coated glasses for photovoltaic panels and is also investigating the laser treatments of semiconductor materials for possible use in electronics. One related product growing out of this type of research is a solar roof panel, which is soon expected to be available for automobiles to help charge the battery and run small fans and other units while the vehicle is parked.

Toledo-area economic development planners are also continuing to study the region's automotive-

Another surprise development has been the opening of Japanese-owned plants within easy reach of Toledo. Toyota, Honda, Mazda, and Nissan all have factories located within less than a day's drive from Toledo. A recent study showed that 59 final truck and auto assembly plants, representing 77 percent of North American final assembly facilities, are within 500 miles (or 10 hours) of Toledo. Twenty-seven of these plants, in fact, are within 250 miles of Toledo!

The same study disclosed that Toledo-area companies manufacture what could be considered a major part of an automobile if all the components produced here are added up. The early development of Champion Spark Plug, for example, made Toledo the early capital of that industry. But 11 other auto and truck engine components also are produced in the city. Toledo firms produce 9 important auto trim and interior components, 14 major parts for the body, and 10 chassis components. This is major business, especially now that there's a continuing trend towards out-sourcing on the part of auto and truck manufacturers. It will admittedly be a highly competitive business as auto manufacturing becomes even more global in the next 10 years. But Toledo, with its access to the market and its wide range of auto suppliers and well-trained workers, should continue to claim its share of auto-components manufacturing.

Though Toledo has a large skilled-worker pool, the pay rates in the community are average. The starting pay for engineers, for example, ranges from about $12 per hour to $16. Tool and die makers earn from $10.50 to $15.50 per hour. Here are recent starting pay-ranges provided for other job classifications: machinery maintenance mechanic, $7.87 to $9.80; production worker, $5.26 to $7.16; maintenance repairer, $4.90 to $6.39; machine operator/tender, $6.12 to $9.10; packaging and filling machine operator, $6.83 to $6.90; freight, stock, and material mover, $5.07 to $7.56; machinist, $6.71 to $9.83; and assembler and fabricator, $6.83 to $6.90.

As for the future development of small- to medium-size businesses and manufacturing firms, Toledo has numerous advantages including the availability of 27 industrial parks in or around the city. Firms locating in the Toledo area have an advantage of attractive tax rates ranging between $34 and $55 per $1,000 of valuation. At the same time, the area has an abundance of natural gas, water, electricity, and sewage services, which are available to most of the parks. Many of the industrial parks also have buildings or acreage available.

One SeaGate is 32 stories high and is Toledo's tallest building. It directly overlooks the Maumee River on its southeast side. Serving as the world headquarters of Owens-Illinois, the leading glass-container firm (which has diversified into additional products and services), One SeaGate is also a symbol of a cooperative effort by major Toledo corporations and public

ABOVE: The Big Three American automobile companies have manufacturing facilities in the Toledo area, including the Chrysler Jeep plant near downtown Toledo. Photo by Sue Keyser

FACING PAGE: Downtown Toledo teems with activity during the city's peak business hours. Photo by Sue Keyser

TOP: Promenade Park in downtown Toledo offers a scenic daytime leisure route for the area's work force. Photo by Barbara Durham

FOLLOWING PAGE: One SeaGate features an inviting reflecting pool, which is highlighted by a granite sculpture by Harvard artist Dimitri Hadzi. Photo by Brad Crooks

officials to beautify the downtown area while preserving it as a business center. Completed in 1981, One SeaGate is sheathed with a curtain wall of reflective glass in an attractive blue-green tone. Its retail concourse on the lower level connects by tunnel with other buildings in the immediate riverfront area.

One SeaGate also includes an attractive fountain area with a striking granite creation by the noted Harvard sculptor, Dimitri Hadzi. This open area immediately adjoins the new Mariott Hotel and connects with the adjacent riverfront, which has newly built sportboat docking facilities and pleasant brick and paved walks. Other new buildings recently constructed on the Summit Street riverfront are the Portside festival marketplace and Three SeaGate, a banking center. While the festival marketplace developed economic problems in its first few years, it is an attractive structure that is believed to have important uses in the future.

Other additions in the riverfront section of the downtown include Four SeaGate and Summit Center, both new office buildings, and an enlargement of historic Trinity Church, an 1863 structure that is also a city landmark. Fort Industry Square, at the southeast end of Summit Street, is a development of very effectively renovated older buildings.

The name SeaGate was an obvious choice for Toledo's downtown buildings because it symbolizes the city's access to world shipping via the St. Lawrence Seaway, which was opened in 1959. That made SeaGate Centre the logical name for Toledo's convention facility, which was completed in 1987. Now attracting 100,000 visitors yearly, it faces Jefferson Avenue and adjoins two hotels on Summit Street in the riverfront area. The SeaGate Centre lobby on Jefferson Avenue has a corner section devoted to the Northwest Ohio Junior Achievement Business Hall of Fame. Established in 1988, the hall honors the area's outstanding business leaders—a regional form of the National Business Hall of Fame at Chicago's Museum of Science and Industry.

The largest industrial site in the Toledo area, in terms of total area, is Arrowhead Park, a 1,100-acre complex on the southwest rim of Greater Toledo. Opened in 1977, Arrowhead was designed to be preserved as an attractive business environment while providing buildings for a range of needs: warehousing, distribution, light manufacturing, and administrative and technical offices. When this planned business community was launched, it had only three businesses, with a total employment of 21; today, it has nearly 200

resident organizations with a combined work force of about 9,000—many of them administrative, technical, and professional workers. Yet only about one-half of the total area has been developed, which provides sufficient room for considerable expansion in the high-tech and administrative businesses Toledo hopes to attract in the 1990s. The recent opening of a new interchange near Arrowhead Park for easier access to the Ohio Turnpike (I-80) and U.S. 23 (which connects to north/south I-75) also makes the location even more desirable for employees and customers.

Another highly successful development park is the Ampoint Industrial Complex, located three miles south of Toledo at Exit 197 on I-75 in Perrysburg Township, with convenient access to the Ohio Turnpike. Ampoint provides lease space for use in warehousing, distribution, manufacturing, and assembly and currently has more than 45 businesses in operation at its site. The complex also has more than 14 major buildings ranging in size from 172,800 to 200,000 square feet.

A different sort of an industrial park is the Willis Day Business Center, which was refurbished from a former Dana Corporation factory site in North Toledo. Financed entirely by private funds, the 1.3-million-square-foot structure was remodeled, and a new heating system and loading docks were installed primarily for manufacturers and distribution companies. Opened only in 1987, the center is now 75 percent occupied and President Bill Day expects full occupancy soon. He attributes this to "very competitive rates" with excellent truck facilities and availability of power.

In addition to these, other industrial parks that have been developed to promote the city's future business include the Cedar Business Center, the Oak Openings Center for Industry, and the Port Alexis Industrial Park, which the Port Authority established. Though some of the older industrial parks are now fully developed, there are available sites in various parts of the metropolitan area for every business purpose—and at affordable rates.

Toledo is a substantial market for retail sales, which total about $5 billion annually for the community. Though retail business is often derived from other, more basic commerce, Toledo's development of retail comprises a very important segment of the area's economy— accounting for at least 60,000 of the community's 284,000 jobs. Additionally, the large retail malls in Toledo have become magnets for further adjoining development of offices, independent retailers, and service businesses. Some of this growth has been so impressive that malls a mile or more apart from each other have become virtually interlocked with continuous retail businesses.

The shopping mall development in Toledo has passed through a number of distinct phases. One of the oldest open malls is Westgate, which created a sensation at its grand opening in May 1960. The completion of Franklin Park, about 2.5 miles away, in 1972, appeared to be a threat to Westgate because the Franklin facility, in addition to having important anchor stores, was enclosed with both central heating and air-conditioning for the concourses facing stores. Yet the growth in both locations has been substantial, and the connecting streets now include many businesses opened in the 1970s and 1980s.

The other enclosed malls in the Toledo area are Southwyck (southwest), the Woodville Mall (eastern suburbs), and North Towne (on the far north near the Michigan line). The community also has Miracle Mile on the north and Great Eastern in the east; both are open, L-shaped malls that continue to serve the adjoining community. Meanwhile, there have also been numerous smaller neighborhood shopping centers constructed with retail, service, and professional offices—providing convenience as well as proof that small business firms and real estate developers have confidence in Toledo's future.

In addition to using these suburban towns to establish locations, Toledoans also refer to the large shopping malls: "Out by Southwyck" means somewhere in the vicinity of the Southwyck Mall, which was viewed as something of a development miracle when it was completed in South Toledo in 1972. Promoted by a supercharged developer, the late Dean Bailey, the complex gave rise to a cluster of new businesses in the entire area, as well as serving as the center of a relentless growth that now extends far to the west of the shopping mall. Though Southwyck businesses still prosper, there have been an assortment of smaller neighborhood shopping centers also shoehorned into the area.

Another area is "Westgate" in Toledo's northwest section. The best way to sum up Westgate is to say that it's a great idea with staying power. Opened in mid-1957, the exciting L-shaped open mall with its 40 stores became the first real rival to the downtown retail businesses. As years passed and the new air-conditioned closed malls came into being, there was a suggestion that the Westgate idea had been bypassed. But instead, it has continued to grow and seems destined to contine as a thriving commercial center. What's more, it's now surrounded by other stores and office complexes that make it virtually contiguous with the commercial activity going north on Secor Road and crossing Monroe Street.

There's also the Franklin Park area to the north and west of Westgate, and in fact almost connected to it as a result of development along Monroe Street. An enclosed mall like Southwyck, Franklin Park has also become a center for additional growth surrounding it.

Another enclosed mall is North Towne Square, located near the Michigan border and very close to Point Place, an outlying part of Toledo that faces Lake Erie. Like the Woodville Mall east of Toledo, it was built to serve a large, partly rural suburban area.

Even more proof of retailers' confidence in Toledo's 1990s economy is shown by the recent development of two major "power center" malls in the area. Spring Meadows, on the west side adjoining U.S. 23 and Airport Highway, is one major "power center" closely matching North Towne Commons, on the north side near Alexis and Lewis avenues. The "power center" mall, a local developer explains, has anchor stores, which specialize in market segments rather than the large department stores that usually serve as mall anchors.

These new malls and a number of discount retail firms have created what amounts to another tier of commercial activity in Toledo. The area now has three wholesale clubs and a number of discount retailers specializing in narrow market segments such as toys and office supplies. Meanwhile, another major discount chain has chosen sites in the Toledo area for building five "hypermarkets" that will add one million square feet of retail area to the community. Since most of these firms have been established since 1987, it raised the question: What do these local discount retailers know about Toledo's future prospects that

L SHOES

Keidan's
JEWELERS

Corey's jewel box

Southwyck Mall helped to
establish a new era of business growth in South Toledo
when it was developed by
the late Dean Bailey in 1972.
Photo by Barbara Durham

ABOVE: North Towne Square is Toledo's newest enclosed mall. Photo by Herral Long

RIGHT: Picnic-in-the-Park is a welcome haven for hungry shoppers at the Franklin Park Mall, located at the corner of Monroe Street and Talmadge Road. Photo by Sue Keyser

makes them so willing to lock up massive investments in a market that's not likely to have huge surges in population growth?

Stephen W. Serchuk, a local developer and broker of commercial real estate, explains it this way: "It's a function of Toledo's being a very stable market. A lot of these retailers have been in boom markets, and then what happens is they go bust, like Houston and Dallas and other Southwest communities." He believes that Toledo's trade area population, which was virtually unchanged from a level of about 615,000 all through the 1980s, will maintain at least the same strength in the 1990s. The national discount chains are well aware of this stability and find it desirable, which is why they've chosen Toledo, he believes. He does not expect the new competition to drive established retail firms out of business, but he does believe that the influx of new retail firms will result in lower prices, benefitting Toledo-area consumers.

In assessing Toledo's current economy and future outlook, it becomes clear that there's good reason to believe the community will do well in comparison with other northern industrial cities. It is taking steps to promote its own economic development with plans based on a realistic evaluation of the area's principal advantages. It is doing everything possible to maintain a favorable business climate environment for the larger industrial firms in the area, while accepting the fact that future growth must stem from newer entrepreneurial activities. The community also supports the educational and training facilities needed for true business and industrial growth.

Toledo today has far more general optimism than it did in the early 1970s, when business analysts were predicting doom for most of the industrial cities tagged as "rustbelt" towns. The rust, if it ever existed, is gone today, and there's great confidence that Toledo has a future. The new business, as it continues to grow and develop in Toledo, will also be competitive in the new world markets of the future.

Randall Root:
Champion of Enterprise Renewal

What causes some businesses to grow and prosper while others stagnate and die? Ask this of Randall Root, the 45-year-old president of Root Publishing, and the answer comes laced with powerful, provocative ideas which he views as keys to future success. These are ideas that form the focus of talks and reports he and his associates deliver regularly to more than 25 major corporate clients worldwide, including two in Sweden.

Root, a native of Toledo who graduated from the University of Toledo with a marketing degree in 1968, has sobering thoughts about the business transformation that will hold sway in the 1990s. He thinks many business executives and leaders in communities like Toledo are caught in a mindset linked to the industrial success of the past. This causes them to worship the large factory as the basic provider of jobs and income, when in fact all large organizations are being rapidly downsized. "Driven by information and technology, we're making the transformation into a new era," he says. "This new information and technology will empower smaller businesses, giving them distinct competitive advantages in the future."

Though most of Root's clients are in other major cities, he frequently advises local business groups in speeches and in executive intelligence reports prepared for a Toledo company. He warns that it's insufficient to depend too much on such economic advantages as the city's favorable location near Lake Erie or "brick-and-mortar" assets. Root's main emphasis is on the development of human capital. "Our greatest asset is our dwindling number of bright young people," he insists. "They are the seed corn of the future."

And he adds, by way of further warning: "We've been living in a home largely built for us by legendary industrialists. It's time to build a new home by stimulating entrepreneurship. Here again our young people are destined to lead the way. We must teach them how to create wealth."

Though he believes Toledo has some problems to overcome, he does feel the area has advantages for developing a "core competence" and a "sustainable competitive advantage" for the future. Root views some of Toledo's main strengths as being good family values, a high quality of life, and good educational facilities. He notes that an area's college institutions should also be "world-class" and believes that both the University of Toledo and Bowling Green State University are moving in that direction, while Owens Technical College is also offering vital training for two-year students.

In his recent studies and reports, Root has focused sharply on the role of "time-based strategies" for the 1990s. He's convinced that survival will de-

Photo by Herral Long

pend on a firm's ability to save customers' time, whether it's by reducing the new product development cycle or simply in responding quickly to customer needs. Toledo has a distinct advantage in time-based competition, he says, because it's much easier to get things done here than in many other areas. He notes, too, that Toledo was chosen as a large hub point by Burlington Air Express and United Parcel Service because both are time-based companies who must respond quickly to their market.

Root started his firm in 1977 following experience in marketing and public relations. He was director of public information for the Toledo-Lucas County Port Authority and later became vice-president of Flournoy & Gibbs, a Toledo-area marketing communications firm. His company is now headquartered in the Toledo suburb of Perrysburg. His wife, Deborah, also a Toledo native, is associated with him in the business. They have two young daughters.

CHAPTER THREE

On the Move

For travelers and shippers, Toledo has been a highly accessible city since its earliest days. Even in 1837, when newly chartered Toledo was a village of about 1,200 people, a steamboat named the *Commodore Perry* began navigating the Maumee River and Lake Erie. That same year, 756 steamboats and 203 schooners cleared the Port of Toledo. And by 1850, the construction of waterways brought more than 4,000 canal boats into the port. This port traffic also gave rise to shipbuilding, cargo hauling and storage, and the warehouse industry, according to Charles N. Glaab, a professor of history at the University of Toledo.

Even while the canals were writing a new growth chapter in Toledo, the railroads that would replace them were under development. Toledo had a primitive railroad extending about 45 miles northwest to Adrian, Michigan, by 1836, and the following year this railroad—the Erie and Kalamazoo (E&K)—had its first steam locomotive. Then as railroads pushed west, the E&K became part of the Michigan Southern, forming a route from Toledo to Chicago in 1852. This marked the true beginning of a golden age in railroading that made Toledo even more accessible to the nation's commerce.

Since railroads followed the waterways

From the majestic Great Lakes freighters to the rumbling freight trains, Toledo is truly a vital transportation and distribution center. Photo by Haz Keyser

RIGHT: Toledo's Amtrak terminal on Emerald Avenue offers service to many destinations across the country, including daily service between Toledo and Detroit. Photo by Haz Keyser

BELOW: Five major railroad lines move through Toledo, making the city the largest rail center in Ohio. Photo by Sue Keyser

FACING PAGE: En route to outlying distribution points, these railcars carry a shipment of coal through Toledo's bustling CSX rail yard. Photo by Sue Keyser

in promoting business and industry, it's not surprising that some of Toledo's greatest industrial growth paralleled the completion of the great railway systems. By the eve of the Civil War, increasing transportation services had helped elevate Toledo's population to 18,000. After that, growth was swift. Toledo's population more than quadrupled in the next 25 years and by the turn of the century, 24 railroads served the city.

Transportation and a favorable location were so important to Toledo's growth that by 1912 a writer summed it up thusly:

It is as a transportation center that Toledo stands preeminent. With a very fortunate location, practically on Lake Erie, the city has become a natural terminus for the boats that carry the northern iron ore and the Pennsylvania and West Virginia coal. Six distinct steamship lines make regular trips to Toledo, the passenger traffic being especially heavy in the midsummer months from the large cities in the vicinity. The official figures show Toledo to be practically the leading port on

about the size of Toledo. The electric railroad has only added to the territory that this city dominates in trade circles. A total of eleven roads are already operating and another is in the process of construction. With what the steam lines, the interurbans and the steamship lines, Toledo is possessed of unlimited facilities by which her trade influence can be extended and strengthened.

Though the passenger steamships and the electric railway systems are gone, there's still much in the above description that applies to Toledo. Railroads are, surprisingly, still an important factor in Toledo's transportation systems. Even today, Toledo is the largest rail center in Ohio. Despite the effects of consolidations and restructurings, Toledo still has five railroad companies, including Conrail, CSX, and Norfolk-Southern. Conrail's Toledo Division, with 1,800 employees, is the area's busiest railroad. About 70 percent of the company's national piggyback traffic moves through Toledo. In addition to freight and commodity shipments, Toledo still offers rail passenger service, which may be augmented in the future, according to recent reports.

But railroads are only part of Toledo's transportation network. Anybody who travels or ships products and commodities has a wide range of additional choices. A traveler can still come to Toledo by private boat as well as by highway, rail, and air. A shipper has choices that include railroads, Great Lakes freighters, about 100 trucking companies, and air freight companies operating out of Toledo Express Airport. And Toledo's refineries also make it a hub for pipelines.

the Lakes, for it excelled all other ports in the tonnage of coal shipments and iron ore receipts. Nature helped even more greatly when it placed this city upon the main line of the great trunk lines that connect the seaboard cities with the large centers of the west. A total of twenty-two railroads radiate from Toledo to all parts of the country. Through them the local merchants tap many rich districts, the unusually large number of roads making the radius larger than in the case of other cities

It is the air freight future that has caught Toledoans' attention in recent months. Burlington Air Express (BAX), the second-largest international cargo operator in the United States, is beginning operations at Toledo Express Airport with a new 279,000-square-foot hub facility in which it is investing $50 million. In full operation, the terminal will handle 350 million to 400 million pounds of freight

FACING PAGE: Passenger departures and arrivals at the Toledo Express Airport are expected to total about 700,000 annually before the mid-1990s. Photo by Brad Crooks

ABOVE: The Toledo Express Airport offers attractive and spacious waiting areas for its passengers. Photo by Barbara Durham

TOP: The second-largest international cargo carrier in the country, Burlington Air Express has chosen the Toledo Express Airport as the site for its new hub facility. This new development is creating about 850 jobs for the area's work force and is expected to handle more than 20 air cargo flights every weeknight. Photo by Herral Long

every year. About 850 full-time and part-time jobs are being created by the Burlington development, and the system will bring in about 22 air freight transports every weeknight, while at least 100 trucks daily will be required to relay shipments in and out of the terminal. The BAX Toledo hub will connect with an air transportation network that services all major U.S. cities and about 60 foreign countries, including those in Europe and the Far East.

Why was Toledo selected as the site for this remarkable opportunity? In the view of Burlington's planners, it made good business sense because of Toledo's location and its access to interstate highways in all four directions. Toledo Express Airport has the facilities for major air freight operations, as well as land area for the terminal. Toledo's proximity to Detroit was another factor, and air freight shippers can serve this market more effectively than from the previous hub in Fort Wayne, Indiana.

Yet the Toledo facility can operate at a lower cost than similar facilities in other locations, an important competitive factor as pressures continue to grow in the air freight business. One study also showed Toledo to be within 500 miles, or a mere hour by jet transport, of 43 percent of United States and 47 percent of Canadian industrial markets, as well as about a third of the households in both countries.

Another positive step, according to the Toledo-Lucas County Port Authority, is that the entire area encompassing Toledo Express Airport will be designated a foreign trade zone. Port Authority officials explain that a foreign trade zone is an industrial area near or at a port of entry under U.S. Customs supervision, where foreign and domestic merchandise may be brought without the requirement of a formal customs entry. The zone, in essence, is considered outside the customs territory of the United States. Goods in such a zone may be stored, manipulated, manufactured, mixed with foreign or domestic merchandise, and even placed on exhibition; duties are paid only when the goods enter the domestic commerce of the United States.

Other operations at Toledo Express Airport will certainly be enhanced by the addition of BAX. This will simply accelerate an improvement process that has been evident throughout the 1980s. Though

smaller than Detroit Metro Airport, only an hour's drive to the north, Toledo Express Airport has the advantage of being more convenient for local passengers and shippers when proper scheduling is available. And extensive airport renovation, including the addition of jetway-enclosed passenger-loading ramps, attractive passenger waiting areas, and other improvements, have helped Toledo Express share in the recent, steady growth in air travel over the past decade.

Passenger arrival and departure traffic at Toledo Express Airport grew from about 400,000 in 1982 to nearly 650,000 in 1989. Projections show that Toledo Express arrivals and departures may reach 700,000 before the mid-1990s.

The Toledo area also has access to two secondary airports—Metcalf Field in the southeast and Suburban Airport just over the northern boundary in Michigan. Both have facilities for corporate aircraft, private commercial aviation, and other aircraft operations serving business and commerce.

While the BAX addition will bring more trucking into the Toledo area, the city is already known as a major hub for highway transportation. More than 100 trucking firms operate in and around Toledo. Toledo has a key position on the Automotive Corridor, Interstate 75, which runs from northern Michigan to southern Florida. Within the Toledo area, important linkages continue to be completed or studied to facilitate even better access to the all-directional interstate network that intersects close to the city.

Though the trucking industry competes with other transportation services, there is also—according to *Blade* transportation writer Hank Harvey—a growing "intermodal" concept that is binding all types of transport together. Trains, for example, haul trailers on flatcars, which is efficient for long-distance hauling. The truck, however, becomes most efficient for servicing local shippers. Trucks are also indispensable to air freight operations, and nobody even envisions a time when air express can reach into the smaller communities without the availability of highway shipping. And both trucking and rail services are necessary in relaying Great Lakes freight cargoes to and from the Port of Toledo.

This seaport—for the St. Lawrence Seaway connects Toledo to the world's oceans—is operated by the Toledo-Lucas County Port Authority, which also directs area economic development. Port facilities have helped make Toledo a major loading terminal for coal, general cargo, grain, iron ore, petroleum, liquid bulk cargo, and dry bulk cargo.

In a typical recent season, the Toledo harbor will handle about 14 million tons of cargo. This includes about 7 million tons of coal, about 2 million tons of grain, nearly 4 million tons of iron ore, almost a million tons of dry bulk cargo, and one-third million tons of petroleum and other liquid bulk cargoes. The total economic impact of this shipment in the Toledo area is in the range of a half-billion dollars. Moreover, Great Lakes shipping is a business that appears likely to go on as a natural fit for Toledo. And as the *Blade*'s Hank Harvey likes to point out, Toledo has a diversity of cargoes entering and exiting the port. Other major Great Lakes ports such as Duluth are tied to one specific cargo, mostly outgoing.

Toledo-area officials have also shown good judgement in developing an efficient roadway network within and around the city. Results of random interviews conducted a few years ago indicated that

ABOVE: Nearly 14 million tons of cargo are handled in a typical season at the Port of Toledo, including some 2 million tons of grain. Photo by Jim Rohman

FACING PAGE: The Port of Toledo is a major Great Lakes shipping center, connected to worldwide markets via the St. Lawrence Seaway. Photo by Jim Rohman

BOTTOM: A vital link in Toledo's transportation network, the trucking industry provides indispensable service to the area's air freight operations and Great Lakes cargo facilities. Photo by Herral Long

BELOW: Major thoroughfares connect the Greater Toledo area with the rest of the nation, creating an efficient transportation system that has helped to establish the city as a leading distribution center. Photo by Herral Long

Toledo-area people feel that the highways, streets, and bridges in Toledo have, in general, been well maintained and are in good condition. The demands on the system are heavy because Lucas County alone has about 400,000 motor vehicles, and there's also heavy truck traffic on highways that connect with interstates. The local highway system is viewed as serving the community efficiently. It is usually possible, for example, to drive across the city in most directions in 25 minutes or less.

Toledoans also give high marks to the Toledo Area Regional Transit Authority (TARTA), their public transportation system. Founded in 1971 to assume responsibility for public mass transit, its services reach out to many suburban communities.

Employing about 300 persons, TARTA operates 41 bus routes and reports an average ridership of 40,000 per day, half of which are school children. Though TARTA currently serves only the suburban communities that support it with tax levies, there's hope that future changes will make it truly an area-wide public transportation system.

Hank Harvey:
Watching The Wheels of Transportation Progress

In Toledo, nothing that touches transportation news is likely to escape the eye of Hank Harvey, who has covered that beat for *The Blade* since 1978. Though appearing relaxed and casual, Harvey is a hard-working reporter with tenacious attention to detail and a keen ability to spot trends in the early development stages. Virtually every transportation story in *The Blade* carries his byline, and he has acquired an almost encyclopedic knowledge of the field. It's possible that he's currently the area's best authority on the past, present, and future of Toledo as a transport center. Harvey's in-depth series reporting netted him a first-place Ohio Associated Press award for 1989, following a third-place recognition the previous year.

One characteristic Harvey brings to his assignments is boundless optimism about the future of Toledo's transportation businesses: lake, rail, air, or highway. He views Toledo as a transportation hub surpassing other great centers, and he can quickly perceive how any new proposal is likely to fit into the larger picture. When Burlington Air Express began to explore Toledo as an air freight hub center, for example, Harvey quickly analyzed the proposal to show how it would affect other business and transportation in the area.

Harvey thinks that his obsession with the transportation industry may be the result of his family heritage and early upbringing.

Raised in Helena, Arkansas, he grew up watching towboats and barges glide past the city on the Memphis-New Orleans leg of the Mississippi River. Helena was also a railroad center, and three generations of his family worked in transportation: His father was a conductor on the Missouri Pacific Railroad; his great-grandfather, a streetcar motorman; and his great-great-grandfather, a station agent. Harvey's memories of his hometown's railroading are so rich, in fact, that he's currently building a model display of its structures and operations in that

vanished era.

Harvey followed a rather circuitous career path before landing in Toledo as a *Blade* writer. He attended a branch of the University of Arkansas for about two years, studying business administration. Returning home to Helena, he worked on a towboat for about nine months and then took off to attend a radio and television school in Memphis. Armed with a certificate, he found work as a radio announcer in a small Arkansas station and later switched to a larger station in Jackson, Mississippi. In 1955 he came north to become a disc jockey at a station in Lima, Ohio. He finally made the leap to print media in 1960 when he was hired as a reporter on the *Lima Citizen*. Three years later, an offer from *The Blade* brought him to Toledo.

"My initial job was at the regional desk," Harvey recalls, "and then I was on the courthouse beat for about five years." Later covering city hall for *The Blade,* he took time off to attend the University of Michigan on a special scholarship from the American Political Science Association, which he won in nationwide competition. On his return to *The Blade,* his stories on different parts of the Toledo transportation system gradually led to the consolidation of this reportage into one job.

Harvey feels that the growing intermodal practices of transportation—such as rail cars carrying truck trailers and the Port Authority using the trucking business—also made it sensible to set up transportation as a single beat.

"I consider it the most important beat on the newspaper," Harvey says. "There's not much scandal, yet it covers the expressway and highway projects. That's always good for news because there's always work going on and there always will be. We'll never be able to catch up with what needs to

Photo by Herral Long

be done." He also explains that an important part of his job is coverage of the Port Authority and the aviation transportation system.

In addition to his transportation interests, Harvey writes authoritatively on history and music. A musician himself, he plays the bass fiddle in a Dixieland jazz band. Back in his radio days, he was one of the first disc jockeys to spot Elvis Presley's rising talent, and even today he follows the Elvis story as it continues to evolve.

Now one of *The Blade's* senior reporters, Harvey is beginning to think about what he wants to do in retirement a few years down the road. He discovered that he wants to continue writing about transportation, music, and the other things he knows best. And one of his most urgent projects will be to revise a *Highway Handbook* he wrote and self-published in 1981. In it, he traces every U.S. highway from start to finish and describes what's along the way. In typical Harvey fashion, he supplied continuous detail beginning with the fact that the U.S. highway system was started in 1926. There were 193 U.S. highways by 1980, and as he explained, they offered "a chance to get near the real America. You may ford dry creek beds, wait for herds of sheep or buffalo, and smell the honeysuckle vines down south. They offer an often slow, but satisfying, slice of travel the way it used to be."

CHAPTER FOUR

Relaxing and Learning in Toledo

T he humorists who depict Toledo as Dulls-ville haven't taken a real look at what the city has to offer. Toledo is actually a great place for personal enrichment, fine entertainment, and recreational enjoyment. It has something for everybody. It has opportunities for serious students and devotees of the arts. It provides outlets for entertainers, both amateur and professional. It's also a city for sportsmen, sports fans and people who pursue a variety of other recreational activities.

It is part of Toledo's remarkable diversity that it can be a center for the fine arts as well as a city that hosts bowling tournaments and hydroplane races. It owes this rich diversity to its excellent location, to ongoing efforts by many citizens, and to some deeply committed people in its past who devoted themselves to building up important institutions. One outstanding institution that represents Toledo's high standing in the fine arts is the Toledo Museum of Art, which may be the city's best-known cultural resource. Attracting more than 400,000 visitors yearly and ranked with the world's

The wooded trails of Swan Creek Preserve are enjoyed by the entire family. Photo by Brad Crooks

RIGHT: The scenic grounds of the Toledo Museum of Art provide an ideal setting in which to explore the world of fine arts. Photo by Herral Long

BELOW: More than 400,000 art lovers visit the Toledo Museum of Art each year; exhibits include American and European paintings, sculpture, photography, decorative arts, and a renowned glass collection. Photo by Brad Crooks

FACING PAGE: Founded in 1901 by Edward Drummond Libbey, the Toledo Museum of Art offers an impressive collection of paintings and sculptures as well as comprehensive art and music programs for both children and adults. Photo by Haz Keyser

great art museums, it has a collection of over 700 American and European paintings and sculptures. Though it embraces a wide range of interests in the visual and musical arts, the museum's most important current collections are its ancient Greek vases; seventeenth-century Italian and Dutch paintings; eighteenth-century French, Italian, and British paint-

ings and decorative arts; nineteenth-century European and American paintings; as well as glass from 2000 B.C. to the present. The museum offers extensive art and music educational programs, which serve groups ranging from very young children to university students in degree programs. The stately museum building, which is located in Toledo's Old West End, also has a performing hall called The Peristyle where outstanding musical and dance programs are presented during the year.

The Toledo Museum works with other leading museums in presenting special touring exhibitions

of major collections. In 1990, for example, it joined a five-museum consortium, which cooperated in presenting some of their finest Impressionism collections in a single exhibit. The exhibit has 85 paintings and sculptures by 21 of the most celebrated Impressionists and Post-Impressionists, including work by Pissarro, Monet, van Gogh, and Signac.

The Toledo Museum was credited, too, with spearheading the highly acclaimed exhibition in 1982 and 1983 of an El Greco exhibition assembled from leading museums around the world. More than 180,000 people viewed the Toledo's El Greco exhibit, which was displayed in only three other major museums: Museo del Prado in Madrid, the National Gallery of Art in Washington, and the Dallas Museum of Fine Arts.

The Toledo Museum was founded in 1901 by Edward Drummond Libbey, who then served as its president until his death in 1925. Though Libbey and his wife supplied substantial financial support for the museum, it was also their love of the arts that helped shape the museum's future. Even today, funds from the Libbey estates continue to help the museum, though it now draws much of its support from thousands of members and contributors in the community.

Toledo's devotion to the arts, however, goes far beyond the visual and crafted works in the museum collections. If Edward and Florence Libbey were still living, they would be delighted with Toledo's progress in its development of locally based and sponsored performing arts groups, including orchestral, vocal, dance, and theatrical. A good example of Toledo's strength in this area was an early 1990 premiere of *A Midsummer Night's Dream* and *Cole* by the Toledo Ballet Company. Though offered by the Toledo Ballet Association, the Shakespearean fantasy (which is set to the music of Felix Mendelssohn) highlighted 20 Toledo opera singers accompanied by the Toledo Symphony Orchestra under the baton of a guest conductor. All three performing groups have given long and distinguished service in Toledo.

The Toledo Symphony Orchestra is known today for providing a wide variety of about 500 performances a year, reaching about 300,000 listeners at more than 300 locations. Organized in 1943, the sym-

phony now ranks as one of America's great orchestras, with an annual budget of about $2.5 million. Though maintaining a high level of brilliant concerts in classical music, the symphony has progressively broadened its offerings to serve almost every segment of the Greater Toledo community. Its major classical programs are presented in The Peristyle of the Toledo Museum, while other musical series are offered in The Franciscan Life Center at Lourdes College and in the Toledo Masonic Auditorium. The symphony has adopted a policy of "providing something for everyone" in the world of music appreciation, and it offers popular and jazz music, light classics, and Broadway hits as well as old favorites. During every season, a number of highly acclaimed guest conductors and performers appear in symphony performances. Though the symphony is currently classified as a regional orchestra, there's no doubt that the quality of its musical productions is equal to major American orchestras including the Cleveland Orchestra and the Detroit Symphony.

In addition to wide-ranging musical programs from its symphony, Toledo also has three operas staged every season by the Toledo Opera Company. From its inception in 1959, the Toledo opera has maintained

LEFT: This captivating performance of *Guys & Dolls* **by CentreStage Productions at the new Franciscan Life Center at Lourdes College is just one of the many fine theatrical presentations offered in the community. Photo by Herral Long**

ABOVE: Now under the artistic direction of James Meena, the Toledo Opera Company has been presenting quality productions since it was established in 1959. This production of *La Traviata* **was just one of the many great operas to be performed in recent years. Courtesy, Toledo Opera Company**

high artistic standards in productions that serve the best cultural interests of the community while also doing well at the box office.

In the past, main roles in Toledo Opera productions, which are staged at the Masonic Auditorium, were filled by many of the world's leading operatic singers. Under the artistic direction of James Meena, however, these demanding roles are just as often filled by less well-known singers. As one opera associate explained, "James Meena has a network of fellow artistic directors and directors that he uses to pinpoint excellent rising talent. Additionally, we do invite established stars who have performed all over the world." This policy of searching for talented performers throughout the country helps give deserving singers opportunities while also enabling the Toledo Opera to operate more cost-effectively than in the past. And as in the past, the Toledo Opera production casts also include supporting singers from the immediate area.

The Toledo Opera has also expanded its mission of bringing quality musical productions to Toledo. In a recent season, for example, it presented *Tosca, The Merry Widow,* and Verdi's operatic version of *Macbeth.* But it also booked a major Broadway national touring show,

Fiddler on the Roof, in Toledo. And future schedules call for producing American classical musicals locally as well as booking in additional Broadway shows. At the same time, the Toledo Opera will continue to offer a full season of operas and occasional operettas.

In addition to its outstanding offerings in symphonic and operatic productions, the community also has The Toledo Ballet as another leading group in the performing arts. Founded in 1958 by Marie Bollinger Vogt, the Ballet has involved thousands of Toledo young people in the grace and discipline of the dance. While its repertoire includes both classical and contemporary works, the highlight of its season is always the annual production of *The Nutcracker* ballet, with guest artists of national reknown, a singing chorus, and a full symphony orchestra.

Though Toledo books Broadway shows every season, the community has its own amateur and professional groups that offer high-level theatrical performances and give talented actors opportunities in many kinds of productions. While there are a few Toledo theater groups that offer one or two plays yearly, the best-attended plays are staged by the Toledo Repertoire Theatre, the Village Players, and the Westgate Dinner Theatre. Each group has an important niche in the community.

FACING PAGE: More than 200 degrees are offered to undergraduate and graduate students at the University of Toledo, with the majority of these students attending programs in education, law, business, engineering, and pharmacology. Photo by Sue Keyser

ABOVE: Ranked as one of the country's great orchestras, the Toledo Symphony performs for some 300,000 music lovers each year at its more than 500 concerts throughout the Greater Toledo region. Courtesy, Toledo Symphony Orchestra

RIGHT: Local artist Jim Havens poses with one of his highly acclaimed metal sculptures. Photo by Herral Long

The Toledo Repertoire Theatre, which opened in 1933 with a highly acclaimed production of Ibsen's *A Doll's House,* reported early in 1990 that it had produced nearly 350 plays and musicals during its 57 years of operation. Locally referred to as The Rep, this group stages six major performances every season and offers special programs for children.

Since 1935, The Rep has been located at 16 Tenth Street in the downtown Toledo area, in a brick structure that was once a church and is now a comfortable theater with a proscenium stage and seating for nearly 300. Most of its comedies and dramas are presented in this theater, while Rep musicals are now offered in the elegant new Franciscan Life Center at Lourdes College. Toledoans have come to expect a high level of fine acting at The Rep, and they are hardly ever disappointed. Tom Gearhart, *Blade* entertainment editor, views The Rep as the "most imaginative" of Toledo's theatrical groups. "They stage primarily contemporary

drama," Gearhart points out, "and I think they're doing an excellent job."

Many of The Rep's actors and staff workers are also proud of being second-generation members of the company. Carlaine Miller, who has performed in about 30 Rep productions, followed her mother into the group. Miller believes that The Rep, though an amateur group, has a professional attitude. "Lots of theaters are fun," she says, "but with The Rep, being good is fun, which means you're willing to put in the effort to do it the very best you can."

The Rep's close, friendly rival is The Village Players, another amateur group that brings Toledo excellent productions of old and new favorites. A number of Toledo's best actors perform with both The Rep and the Players. The Village Players is located in a playhouse at 2740 Upton Avenue, just off Monroe Street in an area northwest from the Old West End. Seating 192, the playhouse has been warmed with recent outstanding productions of *Working, I'm Not Rappaport,* and *All My Sons* among the five plays it does every season. Norb Mills, who is chairman of University of Toledo communications department as well as president of The Village Players, appears in both Rep and Players

attracts touring groups from many states and Canada. Founded in 1974, the Westgate Dinner Theatre occupies a building, which formerly housed a cafeteria in the Westgate Shopping Center. Now under the ownership of the Bassett family, it specializes in popular musicals and light comedies that are likely to appeal to people on vacation. Typical Westgate productions have been breezy versions of *My Fair Lady, South Pacific, Brigadoon, Kiss Me Kate,* and *Annie.*

In addition to the Westgate, professional actors can also find employment at CentreStage Productions, Ltd., which opened in 1990 at the Collingwood Arts Center in the Old West End. Organized primarily to provide outlets for Actors Equity Association members in the greater Toledo area, CentreStage has produced *Pirates of Penzance* and *Guys & Dolls,* and its organizers hope to establish a permanent base in the community.

Toledo's resources in the arts are closely matched by its outstanding educational institutions, beginning with excellent public school systems both in the city and the suburban areas. The city has several fine parochial schools, strongly supported Christian schools, and a nationally known private institution, the Maumee Valley Day School. And even at the high school level, the Toledo area has several vocational schools as well as the Penta County and Four-County vocational schools, serving students in the larger area.

productions. The major difference between the two groups, he believes, is that the Players is all strictly volunteer, including the directors. While The Rep is also a volunteer organization, it does engage a salaried resident director.

"The basic philosophy of the Players is to provide entertainment at equitable prices," Mills explains, adding that the Village Players is the lowest-priced theater in Toledo. Mills also says, "The general attitude of those involved with the Village Players is a feeling of 'One Big Happy Family'. While there is a drive toward perfection, there is still the attitude of having fun and a realization that it is all volunteer and avocational."

Toledo also has a professional dinner theater which

At the college level, the Toledo area offers students numerous opportunities for following different educational paths without leaving the community. With the establishment of the Medical College of Ohio (MCO) in the late 1960s, for example, Toledo also launched a program that is positioning the community as a regional medical center. In the beginning, MCO was started because Ohio needed an additional medical school to help ease the nation's doctor shortage. Besides training medical doctors, however, it offers programs in nursing, allied health studies, and it is a graduate school for the health fields. MCO's research and technical center supplies services to other hospitals in the region, and its hospital is important

both as a teaching institution and in offering state-of-the-art diagnostic and treatment services.

While MCO specializes in medical subjects, Toledo gives college-bound students many additional options, including college training at the doctoral level at both the University of Toledo and Bowling Green State University.

Once a city college, The University of Toledo (UT) has been a state institution since 1967, and it continues to enhance its standing among Ohio's 13 state universities. UT is becoming a major research institution, for example, and, with increases in both public and private research grants, is attracting important research scientists to its faculty. It has enlarged both its physical plant and its curricula, and enrollment has increased by nearly 50 percent since the early 1970s. The area in the center of the campus, formerly a parking lot with aging barracks from World War II, has been transformed into the Centennial Mall, a beautiful quadrangle with lovely landscaping and a network of walkways that lead to surrounding buildings. Most of UT's main buildings, and particularly those constructed in recent years, are faced with the attractive limestone utilized in University Hall and other earlier

buildings. Two new UT buildings, McMaster Hall and Stranahan Hall, have garnered architectural commendations. And recent or current major expansion projects include the construction of a $16-million student recreation center, a fraternity and sorority housing complex, and the renovation of Glass Bowl Stadium, which increased seating by more than 40 percent.

In total enrollment, UT has 24,000 full- and part-time students, or the equivalent in hours of about 18,000 full-time students. The university has a well-established graduate student program, which offers more than 100 graduate degrees, 21 of which are at the doctoral level. There are also more than 140 study programs for undergraduate students. Though many types of subjects and programs are offered, UT attracts a majority of its students in pharmacy, business, engineering, law, and education.

Bowling Green State University (BGSU), in the pleasant village of Bowling Green about 20 miles south of Toledo, is also a major state university, offering numerous graduate studies programs. Established early in the century as a normal school for teacher training, BGSU had remarkable growth in the years following World War II and today has about 18,500 students.

With 8,000 boarding students, BGSU has the look and atmosphere of a "public Ivy"—a state university offering high-quality education at reasonable fees with a rich campus life.

BGSU has 14 departments granting doctoral degrees in a total of more than 60 specializations. The university offers 70 master's degrees and 170 undergraduate programs. BGSU has retained its traditional focus on teacher education and is currently ranked among Ohio's leading teacher-training institutions. The university's greatest student attractions may be its College of Business Administration and the College of Arts and Sciences. In the latter college, the popular culture and photo-chemical sciences programs have become very well-known in the academic field. The colleges of musical arts, health, and human services are also outstanding. While the construction emphasis at BGSU has been to renovate, expand, and refurbish older buildings, the university has completed a physical sciences building that includes a 110-seat planetarium and a rooftop astronomy observation unit. The focal point of the entire university, of course, is its Jerome Library, with more than 4 million books, journals, periodicals, microforms, government documents, and other materials.

UT and BGSU are close rivals, but each has specific advantages depending on student need. Though UT has students living on campus, it is often considered an ideal "commuting" school for Toledo-area students who live at home. And while BGSU has students who commute from home, it is viewed as primarily a

ABOVE: Research and development in the plastics field is supported by the Polymer Institute at the University of Toledo, where an extensive selection of engineering and technologies majors are offered in the polymeric sciences. Photo by Brad Crooks

FACING PAGE: Named in honor of glass pioneer Michael J. Owens, Owens Technical College in Rossford offers associate degrees in a variety of technical fields and also helps to meet the training needs of Toledo's growing business community. Photo by Brad Crooks

TOP LEFT: Bowling Green State University currently enrolls about 18,500 students in more than 200 undergraduate and graduate programs at its scenic campus, located just 20 miles south of Toledo. Photo by Brad Crooks

Nearly 2,000 animals of 400 exotic species of mammals, birds, reptiles, and amphibians can be seen at the Toledo Zoo, which also features a conservatory, botanical gardens, and the new African Savanna. Photo by Haz Keyser

boarding school. Both schools have excellent athletic programs and are members of the Mid-American Conference.

Owens Technical College, in the Toledo suburb of Rossford, is a state-assisted school established to respond to the community's technical/retraining needs. "Its name honors, quite properly, Toledo glass pioneer Michael J. Owens, whose innovations brought glass-making into the twentieth century," a local historian noted. "And though Owens himself had only five years of formal schooling, he continued to study all of his life and would have supported the concept of specialized technical training."

At any time, Owens Tech will have employees of nearly 100 local companies enrolled in training programs. Offering associate degrees in many technical fields, the college enrolls about 5,000 students and reports a high degree of job placement for its graduates. The school places 98 percent of its students and 92 percent of them are in their chosen fields. The availability of OTC and its training programs are also considered to be an important asset enhancing the community's ability to attract and retain industrial companies.

Other schools in the Toledo area include Lourdes College, a liberal arts school offering baccalaureate degrees; Findlay College, Findlay, Ohio; Tiffin University and Heidelberg College in Tiffin, Ohio; Defiance College, Defiance, Ohio; Ohio Northern University, Ada, Ohio; Bluffton College, Bluffton, Ohio; Hillsdale College, Hillsdale, Michigan; and Siena Heights College, Adrian, Michigan. Private college education and training are also offered at Davis Business College and Stautzenberger College in Toledo.

In addition to its outstanding cultural and educational attractions, Toledo has beautiful parks and other recreational facilities. Both visitors and residents are attracted to the Toledo Zoo, which must be considered one of the community's most successful restoration efforts of recent years.

Located on 30 acres near the Maumee Riverfront in South Toledo, the city-operated Toledo Zoo in the

RIGHT: Wild deer and other woodland creatures can be seen throughout Toledo's nine Metroparks. Photo by Barbara Durham

FACING PAGE: Ohio's only sand dunes can be found at Oak Openings Preserve. Covering more than 3,500 acres, this park is the largest of the nine Metroparks in the Toledo area. Other park attractions include horseback-riding trails, a cross-country skiing area, and numerous ponds and lakes for fishing and general enjoyment. Photo by Haz Keyser

BELOW: A flowering landscape of roses, wildflowers, rhododendrons, and azaleas graces the Toledo Botanical Garden. Host to the annual Festival of the Arts each June and the Folk Festival in October, the garden also has a collection of artists' studios and galleries on its grounds. Photo by Haz Keyser

1970s was in serious financial trouble as a result of the dip in the economy. By 1980 its survival had become a matter of community concern. The turning point was a study that year by the Toledo Area Governmental Research Association (TAGRA), which reached the conclusion that an alternative to city management was needed. Passage of a county levy helped assure the zoo's financial support and provided for new capital improvements. In 1981, a master renovation and improvement plan was launched, and one year later, the Toledo Zoological Society was given responsibil-

within Lucas County. The most exciting new development, however, was the virtual completion in 1990 of the Maumee Bay State Park, the first such facility in Northwest Ohio. Toledo additionally has 24 parks of 20 acres or more, 81 mid-size parks of from 5 to 20 acres and 37 mini-parks. At the same time, the city operates community centers, golf courses, swimming pools, and provides play areas with baseball diamonds, tennis courts, and basketball goals.

The Toledo area's nine Metroparks are patterned after national parks and attract 2 million visitors yearly. There are 6,400 acres within the parks, which provide year-round programs, walks, and workshops in settings that maintain the "natural" habitat. These natural areas in the Metroparks include walking and bike trails, picnic facilities, and ice-skating and skiing in the winter. Many of the parks include other attractions. Wildwood Preserve on West Central Avenue was once the private residence of the Robert Stranahan family and its 36-room Manor House is open to the public. Oak Openings, another Metropark, contains Ohio's only sand dunes, and is the largest of the nine parks. Pearson Metropark features one of the last remaining natural woodlands of the Great Black Swamp

ity for the entire operation.

In this new, largely privatized management, the zoo has been expanded and enhanced. Existing buildings such as the Reptile House and the Bird House have been renovated, and a children's zoo was opened. But one of the most important new projects was the development of an African Savanna, which became fully operational several years ago. Designed to give species a more natural environment, the Savanna was cited by USA Weekend magazine as one of the 10-best environmental exhibits among the nation's zoos for its 360,000 gallon hippoquarium, which provides the best underwater viewing of swimming hippos. The Toledo Zoo participates extensively in many species survival programs and has been highly successful in efforts to breed lowland gorillas.

In addition to its zoo, Toledo has numerous strategically placed parks and recreation areas. The "jewels" of this network are the nine Metroparks

that once covered much of Northwest Ohio, while Side Cut Park has the Fallen Timbers State Memorial and Monument as well as the remains of the Miami and Erie canal locks.

The greatest advance in Toledo park facilities, however, came with the completion of the Maumee Bay State Park, which faces Lake Erie and lies east of the city in Oregon and Jerusalem Township. Established in 1981 largely as a result of persistent campaigning by Toledo-area State Representative Barney Quilter, the park first opened with 281 camping sites. Beginning in 1988, however, the 2,000-acre park began to change as a result of a $30-million appropriation in state funds. Its centerpiece is an elegant 120-room lodge suitable for conventions and major events. It has indoor and outdoor swimming pools, an 18-hole golf course, and tennis and racquetball courts. Another addition is an amphitheater for outdoor concerts and other events drawing thousands of people.

Sports fans also like living in Toledo. Its proximity to Detroit and Cleveland makes it an ideal location for people who attend professional baseball, football, and basketball games. As a home professional team, Toledo has the beloved Mud Hens, a highly regarded minor league baseball team with a remarkable history. In recent seasons, the Mud Hens' major league team affiliation has been with the Detroit Tigers. Its opponents include teams in cities such as Omaha, San Diego, Nashville, Syracuse, and Buffalo, among others.

The Toledo Mud Hens, a member of the 16-team Triple-A Alliance of Professional Baseball, owes much of its current popularity to the late Ned Skeldon, for whom the team's stadium at the Lucas County Recreation Center is now named. Skeldon was a Toledo mover and shaker who revived professional baseball in Toledo in 1965 and later served as Mud Hens president until his untimely death in 1988. Known as "Mr. Baseball" in Toledo, he also created strong support for the Mud Hens by assembling more than 100 business and political leaders who belong to the team's Diamond Club and help assure the club's financial success. Gene Cook, the Mud Hens' general manager, is also a member of the Toledo City Council.

While Toledoans take much pride in today's Mud Hens organization, they can also point to a rich baseball history that goes back to 1883. Toledo fielded a team called the Blue Stockings whose catcher, Moses Fleetwood Walker, became one of the first black players when major league baseball started the following year. The Mud Hens name was acquired in 1896, the first of two pennant-winning years for the team. A "mud hen," team information states, is "a marsh bird with short wings, long legs and 'baseball sense' that inhabits marshes." And beginning in 1902, the team played at Swayne Field, a stadium that was considered one of the best in the minor leagues. During the ensuing years until 1955, Toledo baseball took a varied and interesting path that even included a season in 1927 when the team was managed by the great Casey Stengel. When professional baseball ended in 1955, Swayne Field was transformed into a shopping center that still goes by that name. But the construction of a new stadium in 1963 and Skeldon's persistence brought the Mud Hens back to active play—and it's Toledo's hope that they're in for a long run.

ABOVE: Pictured here during pre-game warm-ups at the Lucas County Recreation Center stadium, the Triple-A Toledo Mud Hens have received strong community support and peak attendance since they began their affiliation with the Detroit Tigers in 1986. Photo by Brad Crooks

FACING PAGE: Situated east of the city along the shores of Lake Erie, Maumee Bay State Park was established in 1981 and now boasts more than 280 campsites, a handsome 120-room lodge, and a bounty of recreational facilities. Photo by Haz Keyser

Along with supporting baseball, Toledo has an additional reputation for being a great bowling city. This enthusiasm for bowling, along with its excellent location for travelers, made it one of the cities considered some years ago for the Bowling Hall of Fame. Although this permanent exhibit went to St. Louis, knowledgeable people in bowling still rank Toledo with Detroit, Milwaukee, and St. Louis as one of the top bowling cities in the nation. Since the 1960s, the 60-lane Imperial Lanes center on West Central Avenue has hosted the national Professional Bowlers Tour, which is sponsored by Society Bank and televised nationally. Toledo has 20 other bowling centers, including the 64-lane Southwyck Lanes, Interstate with 40 lanes, and the Glass Bowl with 36 lanes. In addition to the annual PBA tournament in March, Toledo centers host numerous regional, state, and local bowling events.

In addition to bowling as both a participatory and spectator sport, Toledo has become a center for the annual World Cup amateur wrestling event. This was launched in 1973 by the late Joseph R. Scalzo, Sr., who was an attorney with Sun Oil Company in Toledo.

BELOW: Outdoor enthusi-
asts have discovered that
the Toledo area is a virtual
boaters' paradise. Photo by
Haz Keyser

RIGHT: Toledoans of all
ages enjoy the many
recreational activities and
resources that abound
throughout the city's more
than 145 public parks.
Photo by Haz Keyser

Working with Milan Ercegan of Belgrade, Yugoslavia, president of the International Amateur Wrestling Federation, Mr. Scalzo established Toledo as the host city for team-versus-team wrestling between a number of European, Asian, South American, and Pacific Rim countries. Even before the Cold War thawed, Toledo amateur wrestling fans had developed a great affection and admiration for wrestlers from the Soviet Union, Cuba, and Hungary, who competed every spring in John F. Savage Hall at the University of Toledo. Mr. Scalzo, whose name was synonymous with amateur wrestling in Toledo, died in 1986 while attending a world championship wrestling banquet in Budapest, Hungary, but the World Cup competition continues under the guidance of his son, Joseph R. Scalzo, Jr., who is also an attorney.

While athletic events and participation attract many people to Toledo, the area around the city is very close to paradise for people who love fishing and boating. Fishing has had a great revival in the past 20 years as Lake Erie has become cleaner and the once scarce walleye have returned by the millions. "The Western Basin is the hottest part of Lake Erie fishing," one sportsman observes. "Between the first part of April and the last of September, it's great for walleye. You can also do well with perch, white bass, catfish, crappie, and both largemouth and smallmouth bass." Another early spring rite in the area is wading and fishing when walleye are spawning in the rivers. Motorists crossing the bridge between the villages of Maumee and Perrysburg will see hundreds of fisher-

men casting for walleye in the river below, and the same activity goes on in the Portage and Sandusky rivers to the east.

Along with splendid fishing, including ice fishing in the winter, the Toledo area offers excellent boating. The great advantage of Western Lake Erie (also called the North Coast) is the availability of docking and port facilities. Toledo has downtown docking for boats, while the area also has hundreds of other places from which boats can operate. The famous Erie Islands, off Port Clinton about 40 miles to the east, are particularly attractive and provide docking for thousands of pleasure boats and yachts in the summer months. In addition to private marinas, there are many public launching sites for boats, and it's not unusual to see boat trailers on the Lake Erie shores from states like Iowa and Kansas. On some days in the summer, a person can observe hundreds of boats in a single five- or six-mile area on the lake.

So it turns out that Toledo people have lots of things to do when they aren't working at making a living. Over the years, some humorists have had a good time portraying Toledo as Dullsville. That gave John Denver's "Saturday Night in Toledo, Ohio," some credibility. But as John Denver himself has discovered during several very successful appearances in the city, Toledo has much to offer as a center for entertainment, enrichment, and all-round enjoyment.

Jim Ravin:
A Blending of Art and Science

Graduating from The University of Michigan in 1964 with distinction and honors in art history, Jim Ravin easily could have chosen to pursue an advanced degree and a professorial career in the same field. Instead, he followed his father into medicine, and today is a surgical director of The Eye Center of Toledo, a regional referral center recognized for the treatment of eye disease. He has been chairman of ophthalmology at St. Vincent Medical Center and is a clinical assistant professor in ophthalmology at the Medical College of Ohio.

But Toledo, and the world, did not lose an art historian in order to gain a talented eye doctor. Drawing upon his background in both medicine and art, Dr. Ravin has attained prominence with his articles and presentations about the diseases of famous artists. He is widely recognized as an expert on that subject, and writers now pay him the compliment of quoting his work. His authoritative, well-documented articles have been published in medical journals, and he has been invited to speak about famous artists' health problems at medical schools and the National Institutes of Health in Washington, D.C. If the ailments of the great artists become a more important part of future art history, it could well be the result of Ravin's work.

Though Ravin has discussed the health problems of past masters such as Rembrandt and El Greco, one of his most publicized analyses concerned the visual problems of the great French Impressionist, Claude Monet. Monet lived well into the current century and received some of the benefits of modern medicine.

Writing in the July 19, 1985 issue of *JAMA* (the Journal of the American Medical Association), Ravin noted how Monet's cataracts had altered the colors of his paintings later in his career and had caused him to become so dissatisfied with his work that he destroyed many pieces. Ravin, during a visit to Paris, examined the medical records of Monet's cataract operations and reviewed the processes that finally re-

Photo by Herral Long

stored his vision, enabling him to recover much of his former color perception. Ravin also wrote about the visual problems of Mary Cassatt, an Impressionist who was a contemporary of Monet, and Edgar Degas, who was legally blind for the last two decades of his life.

As a surgeon who has seen many advances in ophthalmology, Ravin also notes in his commentaries how modern methods could have helped many of the great artists. Though Monet was fortunate in having ophthalmic surgery, Ravin noted that it would have been better for the great Impressionist if he had been operated on today. "Monet's cataract would be out, he'd have an implant, and he could be back at work the same day," Ravin said in a talk before the American Academy of Ophthalmology in New Orleans. "The odds are that he'd also be back at top form. Just think what art we may have missed."

In addition to his interest in art history, Ravin and his wife, Nancy, are devotees of Sherlock Holmes. Ravin is also an expert on the works of Sir Arthur Conan Doyle, who was an ophthalmologist before he began producing his great stories about the Baker Street sleuth. Some years ago, Ravin profiled two visits Doyle made to Toledo in 1922 and 1923.

While his practice at The Eye Center

and a heavy surgery schedule make demands on his time, Ravin has volunteered for special medical missions to the Dominican Republic, Pakistan and mainland China. In the Dominican Republic, he joined other physicians in providing medical services to indigent people in a remote village—an experience he found so personally satisfying that he wants to carry it on in other countries. On a proposed China trip, one of Ravin's three daughters has decided to accompany him, and will teach English in the village where he will practice.

Following his graduation in art history, Ravin enrolled at the University of Michigan medical school, receiving his medical degree in 1968. He completed an internship at the Los Angeles County/University of Southern California Medical Center and then returned to the University of Michigan Medical Center for a residency in ophthalmology. After duty as an Air Force flight surgeon, he practiced briefly in San Diego before deciding to return to Toledo, his hometown. To people who find it hard to believe that he chose Toledo over San Diego, he has a simple answer: "I've been to lots of places in the world, and this is where I want to live and work."

CHAPTER FIVE

Toledo Reflections

L ike Los Angeles and San Francisco, Toledo is a port city with a Spanish name. And also like these great cities, many ethnic groups contributed to Toledo's growth. Today its diverse ethnic base is well-recognized in the Greater Toledo community and is a source of growing interest.

Toledo's International Park, an area directly across the Maumee River from downtown Toledo, is symbolic of the community's ethnic diversity. Dedicated in 1981, the park encloses a circular boat basin that includes paved walkways and attractive sitting areas with an excellent view of the Toledo skyline. There are also 26 flagpoles in the park, presented by representatives of many of the ethnic groups in Toledo. The park is maintained by the city's parks and forestry division.

There are believed to be about 80 ethnic groups in Toledo, according to the International Institute of Greater Toledo, though some such as recently arrived immigrants from Liberia have only a few hundred members. Some groups, like the French and English, helped establish the early settlements along the Maumee River that became the city of Toledo. Others came later, many in waves of migration that were of great importance in the growth of the United States. A number of the groups strive diligently to maintain an

Toledo's quiet summer afternoons are filled with an atmosphere of small-town charm and community spirit. Photo by Herral Long

ongoing ethnic identity while others unite only for annual festivals and similar events.

As an early settlement directly on a main route to the West, Toledo attracted a large number of European immigrants. Immigration was so much a part of Toledo's past, in fact, that eight of its mayors have been foreign-born: Alexander Brownlee (1857-1860), William Kraus (1869-1871), Guido Marx (1873-1879), Jacob Romeis (1879-1884), George Scheets (1884-1885), Vincent J. Emmick (1891-1893), Samuel M. "Golden Rule" Jones (1897-1994), and Robert Finch (1904-1905).

In total population, the Toledo metropolitan statistical area is listed in the most recently available census (1980) as about 85 percent white and 15 percent black, Asian, and other groups. The largest single ethnic group in the Greater Toledo area is German, with more than 100,000 members. Other large groups include blacks (65,500), English (42,000), Polish (33,000), Irish (20,000), French (8,300), and Hungarian (7,300). Toledo's Hispanic population was just under 11,000 in the 1980 census, but it may be much larger when the 1990 results are tallied. The Asian population also may have increased. The census re-

port notes, too, that more than 250,000 people in the area claimed mixed ancestries, mostly across European lines.

In many cases, factory employment opportunities drew members of each ethnic group to Toledo. Toledo's population surged from about 30,000 in 1870 to 132,000 at the turn of the century, a 30-year leap that parallels a large national influx of immigrants from Germany, Poland, and Hungary.

Local historian Tana Mosier Porter referred to some of these population surges in "Toledo Profile," published by the Toledo Sesquicentennial Commission as the city celebrated its 150th birthday in 1987. The number of German-born persons in Toledo doubled between 1880 and 1890, Porter noted, but then increased by less than 1,000 people in the next 10 years. This corresponds to what is known generally about German immigration, which declined sharply as economic conditions in Germany improved late in the last century. The period between 1880 and 1900 also brought increases in Toledo's Polish and Hungarian populations, which continue to be highly visible groups in Toledo today.

Porter pointed out that one factory on Front Street, National Malleable Castings Company, em-

LEFT: Spectacular Fourth of July festivities attract thousands of participants and spectators to the colorful Toledo waterfront each year. Photo by Haz Keyser

BELOW: The Northwest Ohio Rib-Off, held in downtown Toledo's Promenade Park, is a must for all barbeque enthusiasts. Photo by Sue Keyser

FACING PAGE: International Park features the colorful flags of 26 nations, illustrating the ethnic diversity of Toledo's multicultural population. Photo by Brad Crooks

ployed many of the Hungarians who arrived in Toledo between 1880 and 1900. "They settled nearby in a community known as Birmingham," she writes. She adds that St. Stephen's Hungarian Catholic Church was organized in 1898 and that Protestant services started that same year evolved into the Magyar Reformed Church in 1901. The "Birmingham" name is still employed today to identify the same area.

Porter explained that churches also were established by Polish immigrants, who settled in the LaGrange Street area beginning in the 1870s, and around Nebraska Avenue a few years later. "Lagrinka," a popular nickname for the LaGrange Street section, is supposedly a Polish-language version of "Lagrange," but it's more likely a term of local coinage.

St. Hedwig's Catholic Church, on LaGrange Street, and St. Anthony's on Nebraska, owe their origins to the late nineteenth-century period of Polish immigration. Leonard Szyperski, a 79-year-old widower who grew up in the LaGrange Street area, believes that Lucas County now has at least 12 Catholic church parishes of predominantly Polish membership. He remembers that St. Hedwig's had

so many activities in early years that "you didn't need any money to have lots of fun." Mr. Szyperski, whose father came from Poland in 1872, says that factory employment drew young immigrants to Toledo. It was often necessary to supply interpreters in the early factories for large groups of workers who could not speak English, he says.

Though the 1980 census listed the Polish population at 33,000, it's believed that about 70,000 people in the area claim some Polish ancestry. LaGrange Street is still the center of Polish activity, but descendants of the earlier immigrants now live in most other neighborhoods. The one event that is almost like a homecoming, however, is the Annual LaGrange Street Festival in July. The Polish Day Annual Picnic is rich with ethnic food, costumes, music, and dancing in the Old Country traditions.

The business leaders who set the pace for Toledo's early growth reflected Toledo's early ties to England and mainland Europe. Edward Drummond Libbey brought his glass company to Toledo from New England, where his English ancestors had settled in 1630. His innovative associate, Michael J. Owens, was Irish, though not from the large group of Irish workers who, Porter says, came to Toledo to work on canal construction beginning in 1832. Henry Spielbusch, a German immigrant who opened a blacksmith shop in Toledo in 1850, is still remembered by a downtown street name, though his firm has disappeared into history. Peter Gendron, perhaps the leading wheel and bicycle manufacturer of his time, was of French-Canadian descent. A bit later on, Robert and Duane Stranahan, brothers of Scotch-Irish origin, brought their Champion Spark Plug Company to Toledo to serve the fast-rising auto industry.

The opportunities were far more limited for most of the early blacks who came to Toledo, as well as for Hispanics who arrived much later. While Toledo does not currently claim to be free of racial disagreements and prejudice, the issues are openly discussed in the community.

William Brower, an associate editor of *The Blade* who joined the newspaper in 1948 as its first professional black staffer, called Toledo's civil rights "enigmatic" when writing about it in 1987. Though citing much progress in political and employment opportunities for blacks, Mr. Brower said that "changes have been made, but I'm not yet satisfied." Lee Williams, a 44-year-old state auditor who heads the Toledo NAACP chapter, voices the same thought, conceding that blacks have made strides forward, "but we should be at parity now, and we're not."

In the years before 1860, Toledo did have a strong position as an abolitionist community and served as an important way station in the Underground Railroad that helped escaped slaves to freedom. Black soldiers from Toledo also served with distinction in the Union Army during the Civil War. But on the negative side, riots broke out in 1862 when black workers displaced striking whites, Mr. Brower noted. By 1900 Toledo had about 3,000 black residents, but none in positions of prominence.

Most of the gains by blacks have been made since World War II, a time that has also brought a rapid increase in Toledo's black population. About that time, J.B. Simmons, Jr., became the first black elected to city council. Elected at first by a largely black constituency, it was a measure of his popularity—and also the city's changing attitudes—when he later was re-elected five times in city-wide balloting. In 1959, Simmons also became Toledo's first black vice mayor. Though Simmons was defeated in a later election, he continues to be remembered as a pioneering leader in race relations.

Under Mayor Lloyd Roulet, who served from 1943 to 1947, the city established a Board of Community Relations. "For two decades the board sought to keep a lid on seething unrest," Brower said, adding that though it lacked enforcement powers, it "exercised much influence and always worked hard to prevent a breakdown in communications."

Toledo-area Hispanics, another group that continues to raise civil rights issues, can also claim recent gains in local representation. One highly visible spokesperson for Hispanic interests is Margarita De Leon, public relations director of Riverside Hospital. De Leon believes the 1990 census will disclose great gains in Toledo's Hispanic population. "My feeling is that Toledo will reflect the national picture in that we will have a substantial increase in the Hispanic population in the area," she says. She believes it will more than double the 3 percent reported in the 1980 census for the Toledo metropolitan area. She attributes some of this growth to immigration from Central and South America, "because of the political social changes occurring there." She points out, too, that in many of the Spanish-speaking countries, the United States is still seen as the land of opportunity.

About 85 percent of the Hispanics in the Toledo area are Mexican-Americans, followed by an increasing population of Puerto Ricans, Cubans, and Central and South Americans. At one point the Mexican-American population was concentrated in the old South End of Toledo. De Leon believes, however, that much of the population has now spread out to other areas in the city. Mexican-Americans originally came to northwest Ohio as migrant farm workers and railroad employees, but job opportunities have continued to open up in many industries and professional fields. And because the Toledo Hispanic population is largely

ABOVE: Youngsters learn the joys of creativity at the annual Crosby Gardens Festival of the Arts. Photo by Haz Keyser

TOP: An outstanding addition to the city's fire department, Michael P. Bell was appointed Toledo's fire chief in the summer of 1990. Photo by Herral Long

FACING PAGE: LaGrange Street is the center of activity for Toledo's Polish community and is host to the Annual LaGrange Street Festival in July. Photo by Brad Crooks

Mexican-American, the two most important ethnic holidays are Cinco de Mayo (May 5) and Dieciseis de Septiembre (September 16), the latter involving Mexican independence.

One noticeable action trend among Hispanics in the Greater Toledo area has been the formation of organizations devoted to specific issues affecting Spanish-speaking people. IMAGE of northwest Ohio, formed in the late 1980s under De Leon's direction, focuses on education and employment issues and serves as an advocacy group for Hispanics. El Grupo Cultural Latinoamericano is an organization dedicated to the preservation of diverse Latin

cultures. The Northwest Ohio Hispanic Business Association is dedicated to providing the resources and networking to help Hispanic business owners succeed.

Three of the ethnic groups in Toledo trace their heritage to Macedonia/Bulgaria, Hungary, and Greece. Though somewhat related in religion and customs, they still strive to maintain individual identities.

Pando Pappas, a director of the Bulgarian-

RIGHT: With the support of three major cycling organizations, Toledo is an active center for bicycling fans. Photo by Sue Keyser

FACING PAGE: Undaunted by the rain, these avid runners take part in Toledo's annual 10K Blade Run. Photo by Haz Keyser

BELOW: The Annual Toledo International Regatta is a popular springtime sporting event. Photo by Sue Keyser

Macedonian Cultural Center in the Toledo suburb of Oregon, believes there are now about 200 Bulgarian and Macedonian families in the area. Most of the Bulgarians arrived in Toledo to work on the railroads and settled in East Toledo, where some Bulgarian families still reside today.

The center was originally established by the Bulgarian Cultural Society to provide practice space for kitka dances and various social gatherings involving the Bulgarian-Macedonian community. Pappas acknowledges, however, the difficulty of maintaining a strong ethnic identity as the older generations pass on and younger members marry into other groups.

Though Toledoans of Eastern European descent maintain ethnic ties through festivals and other social events, the native languages are not widely used today in the community. Donna Petcoff Watson, an outstanding Toledo water media artist whose paintings are offered by major galleries, has warm memories of living in Bulgaria as a young child and later in a Bulgarian neighborhood in East Toledo. "We

spoke Bulgarian almost exclusively at home," she said, "until my parents began to feel that this was a detriment to me." The family also attended a primarily Bulgarian church and was active in Bulgarian-Macedonian activities. This waned in later years, however, and she also lost most of her fluency in the Bulgarian language. But a number of Toledoans still retain close ties to their Bulgarian roots, and some came here as refugees from Communist oppression in their native country.

Toledo's Hungarian immigrants had settled in an area on the east side of the Maumee River that is still called Birmingham. A number of events have continued to draw attention to Toledo's ties to Hungary. Hungarians had fled Communist oppression, but the most dramatic event—and one that brought many immigrants to Toledo—was the Hungarian revolution in late 1956. According to Tana Mosier Porter, Toledo welcomed about 300 Hungarian refugees in 1956 and 1957. One who arrived as a young boy with his family was Peter Ujvagi, now a Toledo machine-shop owner as well as a prominent political leader and a longtime member of city council.

Toledo also has a small, but active, Greek community, estimated at about 400 to 500 families. Most of the earlier Greek immigrants were attracted to the city by factory work, and a few opened restaurants and other businesses, which helped establish a Toledo tradition. One strong bond is the tie to the Holy Trinity Greek Orthodox Church. The highly publicized Greek-American Festival held every fall near the church also serves as a reminder of the community's Greek heritage.

Toledo's largest group, more than 100,000 persons of German descent, has several societies that promote some unity and cultural appreciation related to their ancestry. The major event for this group is Toledo's annual German-American Festival in August, an event that includes seven German organizations. Much of Toledo's German immigration occurred in the nineteenth century, and some of the early German settlers came out of Cincinnati as a result of the building of the Erie Canal. Early Toledo also had a number of breweries established by Peter Lenk and other German immigrants, and these drew many Germans to Toledo for work.

Cincinnati was also the early American source for Toledo's first Jewish

settlers, who were predominantly from Germany. (One legend has it that the name Toledo, which came from the Spanish city, was derived from the Hebrew *toledot*, a word connoting history and generations.) According to the Jewish Federation of Greater Toledo, a large number of Jewish settlers in those years made their living as peddlers, supplying goods to outlying farm areas. Many also made and sold clothing, as well as lent money. By the 1860s, the community's Jewish population had risen to about 200 and congregations were forming for Jewish religious services. Today, Greater Toledo's Jewish population is estimated at 6,300, and the city has three major synagogues representing the orthodox, conservative, and reformed branches.

Early Toledo also had its own Marx brothers—Emil, Guido, and Joseph—who arrived after the 1848 German revolution. All three had successful careers, with Joseph holding an important government post under Abraham Lincoln and Guido becoming mayor of Toledo in 1875. (Other Jewish mayors of Toledo were William Kraus, elected in 1869, and Cornell Schreiber, who served from 1918 to 1921.) Other Jews have made important contributions to the business, professional, and educational life of the community. One of the most influential may have been Jacob Lasalle, who served in the Union Army during the Civil War and then became a partner and president of Lasalle & Koch, one of Toledo's leading department stores for many years.

LEFT AND FACING PAGE: A celebration of the arts and community pride, the spirited ToledoFest is a special Labor Day weekend street fair. From musical performances and delicious food to handicrafts and games of skill, this festival is a favorite summertime event. Photos by Haz Keyser

BELOW: The Jewish Community Center is a focus for year-round activities and events. Photo by Herral Long

Lasalle & Koch's was already a flourishing department store in the 1890s when the first Lebanese immigrant arrived in the city. His pantaloons were so unusual that his first job was posing in the Lasalle's window. But it's said that he found more productive employment later on, with his son becoming Toledo's first aviator.

This early showmanship may have been a favorable omen, however, because two of Toledo's best-known sons in the entertainment world, Jamie Farr and Danny Thomas, are of Lebanese descent. Growing up in Toledo, Jamie Farr was a high school honor

Toledo's active Greek-American community celebrates its heritage every autumn with the crowd-pleasing Greek Festival. Lively entertainment and tempting culinary delights are enjoyed by all. Photo by Sue Keyser

student, hardly a person expected to become the dizzy Corporal Max Klinger of the long running M*A*S*H television series. As part of his M*A*S*H act, Farr helped publicize one of Toledo's outstanding restaurants, Tony Packo's, famous for its Hungarian hot dogs. And long before Farr became a celebrity, Toledo also took pride in Danny Thomas, who was raised in Toledo's Old North End and sold candy at the Empire Theater. Thomas later became popular as a local master of ceremonies before finding his niche in the entertainment field.

Most of Toledo's Lebanese people, now estimated at about 5,000, are descendants of immigrants who arrived in the community after World War I. Many were fleeing the distressed economic conditions in their homeland. While the older Lebanese immigrants belonged to Orthodox and Catholic churches, more recent arrivals are primarily Moslem. One result of this change has been the completion of the attractive new Mosque at the junction of I-75 and I-475, south of Toledo.

Immigrants from various Asian countries also have settled in Toledo in the past two decades. Any listing would now include people from India, Pakistan, Vietnam, South Korea, Japan, China, and Indonesia, as well as other Asian countries. The International Institute, which counsels immigrants and assists them in completing the naturalization process, notes that a wide range of Asian countries are included among the more than 300 persons in Northwest Ohio who are naturalized annually as U.S. citizens.

As a community with roots in many countries, Toledo also has outstanding restaurants with specific ethnic identities. In addition to the Hungarian origins of Tony Packo's Cafe, a number of establishments have ties to ethnic groups within the community. Mary Alice Powell, *The Blade*'s food editor, has noted some of the following: The Beirut Restaurant & Lounge (Lebanese); Sakura Gardens (Japanese);

Theos Taverna & Greek Restaurant; Manos Greek Restaurant & Upstairs Bar & Grill; Byblos Restaurant (Lebanese); Casa Di Maria Restaurant (Italian); Ventura's (Mexican); Thai Guy (Thai); Jing Chuan (Chinese); and Ming's Dynasty (Chinese).

What's the future for ethnic diversity in Toledo? As a port city with transportation and communications links worldwide, the outlook is that Toledoans will continue to become more interested in their own ethnic roots and ties to other countries. Many of Toledo's leading companies have become more international, a trend that will continue into the next century. Libbey-Owens-Ford Company, for example, maintains two flagpoles on the plaza of its headquarters in downtown Toledo, and regularly displays flags representing business visitors from other countries. And like all major state universities, the University of Toledo and Bowling Green State University have large numbers of foreign students and scholars as well as specific international programs. And just as earlier ethnic diversity helped make Toledo what it is today, so should the new international outreach enhance its future growth.

TOP: The stately new Mosque in Perrysburg, built by the growing Moslem Lebanese community, is silhouetted against the early evening sky. Photo by Herral Long

ABOVE: The ethnic diversity of Toledo's communities is apparent in the city's varied cuisine. Lebanese, Hungarian, Polish, and Chinese are just a few choices that Toledoans enjoy. Pictured here is the Manos Greek Restaurant & Upstairs Bar & Grill, which features fine Mediterranean fare. Photo by Herral Long

Nancy Packo Horvath:
A Legacy of Luck and Hard Work

Born and raised in Toledo's Birmingham section, a predominantly Hungarian neighborhood, Nancy Packo Horvath began to learn about the restaurant business while still a toddler. Later she worked in the cafe that her parents, Tony and Rose Packo, had launched in 1932 using $100 borrowed from relatives.

Nancy Horvath, an attractive, good-humored woman of 58, thinks they've had wonderful luck over the years. Tony and Rose, both children of Hungarian immigrants, were lucky in their early choice to offer a special hot dog using a sauce of Tony's creation. Now famous nationally, Tony Packo's Hungarian hot dog is still a centerpiece of the business. It became an attraction for thousands of visitors including celebrities and political leaders. Displays inside Tony Packo's Cafe on Front Street in Toledo include plastic hot dog buns carrying notable autographs including former President Jimmy Carter's.

Along with luck, however, Horvath thinks hard work and long hours were the real reason the business has survived and grown over the years. This capacity for hard work, a legacy from her late parents, is shared by her family associates in the business: her brother, Tony Packo, Jr., and her son, Robin Horvath. Both have key posts in the firm, which operates two Tony Packo's restaurants as well as a growing line of food products now marketed in seven states.

In 1963, however, the responsibility for the business was largely Nancy Horvath's; her father had just died and she found herself in what she describes "as a new ball game," when it was as if "an elephant fell on me." Her brother, Tony Packo, Jr., now president, was then only 15, and she had to take charge of a staff that had previously reported to her father. "Women were not then in positions of control," she remembers, and at one point a number of employees even walked out in a huff when she tried to make a point with them. They returned an hour later, however, and things got better after **that rocky beginning.**

Photo by Herral Long

Horvath also likes to marvel about the lucky decisions that went along with their hard work. In 1964, for example, they decided to decorate the aging building with lamps foraged from estate sales and antique shops. The cafe has become known for its elegant lamps, and one purchased for a mere $200 now has a market value of $20,000.

A second lucky action was the 1967 decision to hire the seven-piece Cakewalkin' Jass Band, which still entertains Tony Packo's customers on weekend evenings. The Jass band is one reason why droves of college students head for Packo's on their weekends back home, but it is also popular with older patrons.

Another lucky break came in 1972 when actor Burt Reynolds autographed a hot dog bun while appearing in Toledo. This started a tradition of celebrity signers that still continues; some persons of note even go out of their way to become Hungarian hot-dog-bun celebrities.

Perhaps the greatest stroke of luck came in 1976, when Toledo-born Jamie Farr (Corporal Max Klinger) mentioned Tony Packo's Cafe and hot dogs in a M*A*S*H episode. This brought an explosion of inquiries from M*A*S*H fans across the country, some from people who wanted to know if there really was such a restaurant in Toledo.

In 1980, the company moved ahead with another plan which, Mrs. Horvath says, is turning out very well. Forming a distribution group called the Tony Packo Food Company, they began marketing the famous hot dog sauce and various pickle and pepper products throughout regional supermarkets. Though moving into a business where the competition for supermarket shelf space is nothing short of deadly, they now have 10 items in the line and have won acceptance in major cities and throughout the Midwest. Nancy Horvath remembers one store that turned them down initially, later giving them their largest order, 1,000 cases for six stores.

Though she now has lots of support from her family members, whom she praises lavishly, Mrs. Horvath still works long hours and has lots of fun developing new ideas for the business. When some critics said the sauce caused heartburn, they designed and sold buttons that said, "I got heartburn at Tony Packo's."

One little-known fact she admits, is that "Hungarian" hot dogs are so-called only because her father created them. No such products are sold in Hungary.

But with Nancy Horvath's marketing, even that could happen some day.

PART TWO

Toledo's Enterprises

Toledo's vibrant economy and
growing business community
are evident in the city's ever-
developing skyline. Photo by
Herral Long

CHAPTER SIX

Networks

T oledo's role as a modern,
thriving metropolitan center
is made possible by its
network of communication
and energy providers.

Columbia Gas of Ohio, 88
WTVG-TV, 89

Photo by J.D. Pratt/
Third Coast Stock Source

Columbia Gas of Ohio

Natural gas was first brought to the Toledo area in 1886 by the Northwestern Ohio Natural Gas Company. Northwestern Natural Gas was a distributor of gas supplied by Ohio Fuel Gas Company, a unit of the Columbia System. By 1930 Northwestern Natural Gas boasted 79,000 customers as people in the Toledo area began to realize the value of natural gas for cooking and heating.

In 1944 the company merged into Ohio Gas and its customer load grew to 83,000. Twenty years later, the Ohio Fuel Gas Company became Columbia Gas of Ohio, with the Toledo region being designated Columbia Gas of Ohio's Northwestern District. Today the Northwestern District has more than 160,000 customers.

Columbia Gas prides itself on being more than just a utility company. It believes that it has a responsibility to the communities in which it does business and has been very active in the areas of economic development and corporate citizenship. Columbia officials work closely with city and state economic groups and local and state chambers of commerce to aggressively pursue new business and industry for the areas in which they operate. The officials take key roles in these efforts because they believe that new business and industry can add vibrancy and an economic boost that will effect a community for decades. The company recognizes the importance of energy supplies to prospective businesses and has proven experience and success in fulfilling the energy requirements of these new companies.

Columbia officials are also key members of the Toledo civic community with leadership experience and representation in virtually all of the area's major nonprofit organizations, including United Way, the March of Dimes, Downtown Kiwanis, and the United Negro College Fund.

Columbia Gas is committed to providing the very best natural-gas services possible at the lowest possible cost. By being a part of the Columbia Gas System, one of the largest integrated natural gas systems in the United States, Columbia Gas of Ohio benefits from the parent company's leadership in research and support technology in developing the most state-of-the-art applications for natural gas.

One of the major areas it is leading the way in is the advancement of gas-powered vehicles. A large part of Columbia's Toledo vehicular fleet is fueled by natural gas and has been for several years. Natural Gas's clean-burning capabilities make it environmentally preferable as a fuel source. Because of this, Columbia Gas of Ohio is actively pursuing the increased use of natural gas for mass transit and commercial fleets.

As more and more attention is focused on the environment and how people must live in ways that cause less damage to the atmosphere and produce fewer pollutants, the clean-burning qualities of natural gas will make it clear in everyone's mind that natural gas is naturally the fuel of the future.

RIGHT: Columbia Gas employees constantly strive to exceed customer service expectations.

BELOW: As a leader in natural gas vehicle technology, Columbia Gas recently introduced "The Columbia," the nation's first transit bus built exclusively to run on clean-burning natural gas.

WTVG-TV

It all began in 1912. That year stories spread of how distress signals from the stricken Titanic were picked up on shore through the magic of Marconi's wireless device. The stories fired the imagination of a 13-year-old Toledo boy. With whisker crystals and spark coils from scrapped Model T's, the boy soon had his own ham radio station operating in the attic of his parents' home. It was the start of a lifelong fascination with the art, science, and business of broadcasting.

The boy's name was George Butler Storer. Commitments to the family businesses, Steel Tube Company of Toledo and Fort Industry Oil Company, kept Storer from following up his interest in radio as quickly as he would have liked. In fact, it was 1927 before he brought his first radio station, WTAL. He bought it because he was advertising his gas stations so heavily on the station that he thought it would be cheaper to own the station outright than to continue to finance it as a major client.

Storer's trade name for the gasoline his stations sold, Speedene, was incorporated into the call letters of his new acquisition, and WSPD was born. During the next 10 years Storer bought five more stations in Ohio and Michigan, and in 1931 he sold the petroleum arm of his business to Standard Ohio of Ohio so that he could concentrate on the business of broadcasting.

After the war Storer began expanding into television with stations in Toledo, Atlanta, and Detroit —a feat unduplicated by an independent broadcaster. The stations were so successful for him that he continued to expand his business, building stations in Cleveland,

Milwaukee, Boston, and San Diego. He also wanted to expand into cable, and to finance that venture Storer Broadcasting sold its radio stations, including WSPD. The call letters were sold along with the station, so WSPD-TV became WTVG.

The desire to serve the community has always been strong at Channel 13. It was the first Toledo television station to present color programs, first with live microwave news capability, and first with five-color weather radar. TV-13 was also the first commercial broadcaster in Toledo with a satellite earth station. The station remains committed to providing quality news and programming to the community.

Creative programming at WTVG includes "Ask the Experts," with leading authorities on such diverse subjects as medicine, law, and home canning; "Call for Action," a consumer help line; and "Wednesday's Child," an effort to get children adopted. The station stresses that these locally produced programs change continually as issues that are important to the community change.

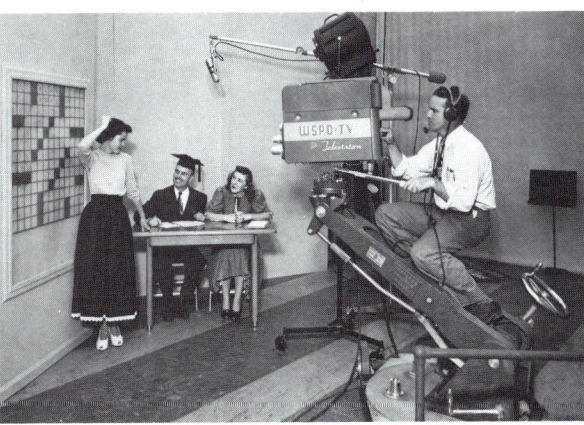

TOP: This beautiful, colonial-style building has been home to WTVG since 1981.

ABOVE: WTVG's early years in broadcasting.

WTVG-TV believes strongly that one of its main roles is to serve the community. It does so through community service as well as specialty programming. Some of the major events it sponsors or produces include the Muscular Dystrophy Telethon, the Holiday Parade during the Christmas season, the Jamie Farr Toledo Classic Golf Tournament, and the Jefferson Awards, a program that recognizes outstanding community service, sending one of five local winners to Washington for national awards.

C H A P T E R S E V E N

Business and Professions

Toledo's professional community brings a wealth of ability and insight to the area.

Shumaker, Loop & Kendrick, 92

Watkins, Bates, Carey & McHugh, 94

Fuller & Henry, 95

Software Alternatives, Inc., 96

Spengler, Nathanson, Heyman, McCarthy
   & Durfee, 98

NFO Research, Inc., 100

The Schroeder Company, 102

Photo by Herral Long

Shumaker, Loop & Kendrick

Shumaker, Loop & Kendrick was formed in 1925 and today is one of the oldest and largest legal firms headquartered in Toledo. It is also the only northwestern Ohio law firm that has out-of-state offices. The firm is composed of more than 80 attorneys in Toledo; Charlotte, North Carolina; and Tampa, Florida, and represents a broad spectrum of commercial, industrial, governmental, and individual clients.

Shumaker, Loop & Kendrick has its roots in a partnership formed in 1896 by two prominent Toledo attorneys, Edwin J. Mar-

shall and Harold W. Fraser. The two were together for 29 years before they each decided to go their separate ways. Fraser joined with six other attorneys to form what is now Shumaker, Loop & Kendrick.

There has been much growth since these early days. "Our steady growth is a measure of our clients' satisfaction," says Donald M. Mewhort, Jr., a long-time member of the management committee. "Experience has taught us that the most effective legal services are based on one-to-one relationships between attorney and client. Such relationships

allow us to identify solutions that can be formulated only by those who have both the law and facts at their command."

He adds, "At the same time, our clients must be confident that we will meet their most complex legal needs, quickly and efficiently. To do this, we constantly strive to make our collective experience readily available to each of our clients by promoting communication within and among our offices."

The firm also believes that regular communication with the client is essential to the success of

LEFT: Shumaker, Loop & Kendrick is headquartered in Toledo and also operates offices in Charlotte, North Carolina, and Tampa, Florida.

RIGHT: In 1985 the American Bar Association Journal awarded Shumaker, Loop & Kendrick its first prize and special award for civic commitment and law office design.

attorney/client relationships. "To provide high quality, cost-effective legal services, knowledge of the law is not enough," says Mewhort. "We must know our clients and understand their business goals, listen and communicate effectively, and be accessible and responsive. Ultimately, our job is to protect our clients' rights, including the right to make their own decisions."

Shumaker, Loop & Kendrick's main practice areas are: corporate tax and securities, which includes mergers and acquisitions, tax counsel, securities law, franchise law, and international law; trade regulation and practice, which includes regulated industries such as telecommunications and transportation, and antitrust law; public law; retirement planning, estate planning, and probate; real estate practice, which includes real estate development, syndications, zoning, land-use regulation, environmental issues and construction law; banking and commercial law, which includes corporate representation, lending activities, and creditors' rights; trial practice, which includes personal injury litigation, commercial litigation, trade regulation, and employment litigation; employee relations law, which includes union organizing, representation elections, NLRB proceedings, collective bargaining, wage-hour, OSHA claims, and

immigration law; employee benefits, which includes representation of multi-employer and single-employer plans; health care practice, which includes representation of hospitals and related entities, nursing, and retirement facilities and practitioners; and environental law.

Quite a list, but one which illustrates the firm's commitment to being broadly based. "We are a full-service operation," says Mewhort, "and the small business or individual is just as important to us as the major corporations we handle. The business climate in Toledo has been changing during the past several years. There are not as many Fortune 500 clients in the area as there used to be. But there are many new small and medium size businesses starting and growing. These types of clients have always been the backbone of our firm. We believe that Shumaker, Loop & Kendrick is positioned to handle their needs."

The firm reaffirmed its commitment to Toledo in 1979 when it announced plans to renovate the plumbers supply warehouse in the Warren-Sherman area near downtown. This project has been hailed by city leaders as a significant contribution to downtown revitalization and development.

A number of the firm's attorneys are active in local, state, and national bar and professional associations, represent indigent clients on pro bono matters, participate in continuing legal education programs and seminars, and serve on boards of numerous civic, charitable, and community organizations. The firm's attorneys were also instrumental in establishing The Toledo Festival of the Arts.

Stability, growth, civic commitment, and optimism about the future of the communities in which it does business is the way Mewhort sums up the firm. "We've been around a long time, and we're well positioned for the future."

Watkins, Bates, Carey & McHugh

Watkins, Bates, Carey & McHugh is a firm with a proud history and an ambitious future. Founded in 1939 by Harley A. Watkins, a distinguished trial lawyer who became one of Toledo's prominent probate and trust practitioners, the firm has consistently emphasized its ability to represent its clients from the boardroom to the courtroom. Its lawyers have developed specialties in many of the emerging areas of law; however, the firm continues to emphasize total client representation. In an era noted for boutiques and single-purpose representation, Watkins, Bates, Carey & McHugh has determined that client interests are more effectively and economically served by well-informed generalists, guided by fundamental values and principles.

Motivated by the philosophy that its lawyers ought to act as counselors first and as advocates only as a last resort, Watkins, Bates, Carey & McHugh represents the small and medium-sized business owner, in both his personal and corporate activities. It acts principally as an outside general counsel, offering guidance on matters as diverse as employee relations, estate planning, and commercial lending. It recognizes that the businessman is best served by a lawyer with a range of talents, one who understands not only the economic environment in which his client competes, but also the significance of his client's enterprise in terms of his employees, his customers, and his family.

Its involvement in counseling smaller clients is enhanced by its experience in representing, as well as in challenging, many of Toledo's largest corporations. Lessons learned in defending lawsuits are carried forward into corporate advice, and insights gained in the boardroom are often carried to tactical advantage elsewhere. Flexibility of representation, whether it be advocating the merits of competing litigant claims or separately acting as counsel to either debtors or creditors, plaintiffs or defendants, provides experience and judgment that enhances client success.

In addition to its regular corporate practice, Watkins, Bates, Carey & McHugh has developed considerable expertise in nonprofit and private foundation work. Guided by a sense of civic responsibility as well as professional interest, lawyers at Watkins, Bates, Carey & McHugh are actively involved in community activities, sit as members of boards of trustees of local hospitals, and counsel various health care organizations and providers. Guided by the admonition that they are judged as much by what they give back to their profession as what they take from it, lawyers at Watkins, Bates, Carey, & McHugh regularly speak and publish on emerging legal issues, participate in instructional seminars and other bar association activities, and teach at the College of Law.

(Back left to right) partners John M. Carey, William F. Bates, Gary O. Sommer, and John J. McHugh III. (Front left to right) Kimberly S. Stepleton, Myna A. Shuster, and Beth E. Beech.

Fuller & Henry

Standing, from left: Fuller & Henry's new 1990 associates Barbarakaye Wright, Scott G. Deller, Joseph S. Simpson, Travis W. Brant, Patrick J. Saccogna, James B. Yates, Kurt J. Lindower, Jeffrey A. Dehner, and Michael J. O'Callaghan. Seated, from left: 1990 managing committee members John W. Hilbert II, managing partner; Louis E. Tosi, chairman; and John J. Sicilian

Fuller & Henry, as it approaches a century of general practice of law based in downtown Toledo, can be characterized presently by its young and vigorous management, rapid growth, and expanding areas of practice. During a developmental explosion, it is maintaining its traditional experienced servicing of all civil areas of law. Its clients are individuals, business concerns, and sometimes governmental units locally, statewide, nationally, and occasionally internationally.

Twenty-five of the firm's lawyers are partners who vary in age from 34 to 69. The average age of the partners is 46 years. Fuller & Henry's three-person managing committee has an average age of 41 years.

The firm's permanent staffing includes 60 lawyers, 11 legal assistants, and 57 non-legal personnel. The growing needs of the firm and its clients are reflected in the 1990 addition of 9 new law graduates to the firm's employed associates, which makes Fuller & Henry one of the fastest-growing law firms in Ohio.

Fuller & Henry's main office is on all of the 17th floor and more than half of the 18th floor of One Seagate and is rapidly expanding. The firm also has offices in Port Clinton and Columbus, Ohio. It is the only Toledo law firm with an office in the state capital. Direct-line computer linkage between Columbus and the main office in Toledo permits full use of all resources from either office.

The firm is fully computerized as to both legal and non-legal personnel. Lawyers and legal assistants can function by computer from their regular individual offices. Typing, recordkeeping, bookkeeping, and billing processes are all computerized.

The firm's law practice has been primarily civil, rather than criminal, in subject. Staffing capabilities for handling all types of civil matters have been constantly maintained; but the volume of activity in any particular field of law varies in accordance with the prevailing problems of the times, locally and nationally. Today the general litigation segment is the largest of the firm's practice groups; and environmental law (in which the firm is a pioneer and acknowledged expert), the law of business and financial transactions, and toxic tort litigation are consuming increasing portions of the firm's practice.

Historically, among the many excellent lawyers who were partners and associates of the firm, three lawyers were preeminent. Chronologically, they were Thomas H. Tracy, George D. Welles, and Fred E. Fuller.

Tracy was one of the two founding partners on April 1, 1892, and remained active in the firm until his death in 1933. Early on he gained national representations that caused the firm's clientele and practice to be widespread and cosmopolitan.

Welles was a dynamic caretaker of the Tracy practice. His precision in performance brought additional representations and opened doors to opportunities for the firm's younger lawyers.

In a career that progressed from general practitioner to general litigator to antitrust litigator to general counsel, Fuller enhanced the firm's representations and reputation. He was a founder and early chairman of the Antitrust Section of the American Bar Association.

A major resource of the firm throughout its history has been its library, perhaps in the present state of art better described as an information (both print and non-print) services center. The central location occupies 4,500 square feet of floor space, includes 23,000 books, and has both Lexis and Westlaw legal research computers, a microforms reader-printer, a photocopy machine, and a video-camera system. Fuller & Henry's library, which extends to satellites throughout the offices and is staffed by a librarian and an assistant librarian, receives unusually wide respect.

Software Alternatives, Inc.

Success, energy, and enthusiasm—you can sense it in the air the minute you walk through the doors of Software Alternatives, Inc.'s headquarters in Arrowhead Park. From the receptionist to the president, this company is on the move. SAI has seen tremendous growth in the last five years and is listed on the Inc. 500 list of fastest growing companies in the U.S.

The company has had average compounded annual growth of 150 percent for the past seven years—it could have grown faster, but the management did not want to sacrifice service. Last year sales topped the $24-million mark. By 1993 company president Joe Links predicts that company sales will exceed $40 million.

In addition, Software Alternatives has been named IBM's number one business partner in the United States for the sixth year in a row. No small accomplishment when 5,000 companies nationwide were in the running.

Links credits Software Alternatives' firm grip on the number one sales position to the aggressive and highly talented computer professionals that the company has on staff as well as the company's commitment to quality service.

"It sounds like an old platitude," he says, "but our clients know they can count on our systems to work and that means a lot in this business. When an organization's computers don't function, business can literally come to a standstill. We've all waited in long lines at the airport only to find that the computers are down. Computers are a very integral part of many companies today so it's critical that the companies installing and programming them are dependable.

"When IBM came to us in the summer of 1983 and proposed an association with them we thought 'this is our big chance,'" Links says, "so we really jumped on it. We were determined to make ourselves indispensable to IBM. And we have."

It is this partnership that has been largely responsible for Software Alternatives' tremendous growth. The first summer with IBM the company installed 700

ABOVE: Joe Links (left) and Bill McGinnis, the founders of Software Alternatives, Inc.

BELOW: One of SAI's training centers.

IBM mid-range computer systems. Last year they installed more than 1,200. "This represents about a $100-million worth of business to IBM," Links says.

Software Alternatives has offices located throughout the United States, serving a growing list of large and small businesses and industries. "While we're constantly adding new clients," Links says, "most of our growth has been repeat business from satisfied customers such as Owens-Illinois, Campbell Soup Company, Beatrice Foods, GTE, Coca Cola, and Marathon Petroleum."

Links sees his company as an extension of its clients. "We get to know them. Find out what they need. Help them maximize their resources, and put all of ours at their disposal. The result is individ-

ual solutions that grow and change as their needs change."

Not only does Software Alternatives keep clients. It keeps employees. Since starting in 1973 they have averaged only a 5-percent turnover rate in an industry that averages 30-percent employee turnover annually. Links believes low turnover keeps the company stable and allows it to attract top-quality people. "This is a people business and it's important that our clients know we'll be here tomorrow," he says.

One of the unique things about Software Alternatives is that the company is headquartered in Maumee, Ohio, rather than in California. "You don't have to live in Silicon Valley to be successful in the computer industry," Links says. He likes the Toledo area because of its central location. "I can be anywhere in the country within a matter of hours. And I don't have to deal with a two-hour commute coming and going from work. The housing alternatives are terrific and the people are friendly and genuine. In short, there is a great quality of life here."

He adds that Toledo also has a fine university with a solid computer program and business school. "It's an asset to have a university of this caliber here because it provides us with a steady source of top-quality employees."

Many of Software Alternatives'

RIGHT: Strategy sessions are frequent at SAI.

BELOW: SAI's state of the art computer room.

meet those needs. With Software Alternatives, however, we believe they get more than a plan. They get solutions. And they get that promise in writing."

The company prides themselves on finding data-processing solutions that work for their customers. "We're with our customers every step of the way," Links says, "until the system they've cho-

gramming services; remote end-user services; technical communications for IBM mainframe, mid-range, and intelligent workstation platforms; connectivity, coexistence, and conversion with non-IBM platforms; technical training; and general networking consultation.

Selecting and installing a manufacturer's hardware is only the first step in a successful computer

sen is fully operational and producing the benefits they expected in the beginning."

As the price and performance of mid-range computers improve each year, many corporations elect to install them in their remote plants, distribution centers, and sales offices. The concept has proven a viable alternative to telephone links or a large centralized computer center. It also provides remote users with a system to address local needs.

Through its affiliation with IBM as a business partner, Software Alternatives has built a reputation as the premier partner experienced in constructing networks among multiple locations. Services include project management skills; custom installation services; contract pro-

clients have become successful by developing innovative, distinctive positions within their marketplace. "We can help them by developing custom computer programs that support and enhance those unique business philosophies and approaches," Link says. "Our consultants are specifically trained to hear a client's needs and to then create a feasible, efficient plan to

installation. It also requires adapting or creating software to the specific needs of a customer's business. And it demands skill in creating policies, procedures, and practices to support the new computer applications.

"Our manufacturing consultants have extensive real-world experience with a client's distinct situation," Links says. "They draw upon more than 60 years experience of private-industry experience as end users or MIS operatives. We're more than just computer people. Each of our consultants has specific expertise—accounting, office, imaging solutions, manufacturing planning, operational tracking and reporting, warehousing, and distribution."

Software Alternatives, Inc., is proud and it has reason to be. It is one of Toledo's new breed of entrepreneurial companies that is alive and growing.

Spengler, Nathanson, Heyman, McCarthy & Durfee

Spengler, Nathanson, Heyman, McCarthy & Durfee has a rich history in the Toledo area, with many of its founders and principals playing key roles in the city's political and business development. The law firm was formed on February 1, 1947, by Otto Spengler, Joe Nathason, Bert Hebenstreit, and Joe Heyman.

Spengler had practiced law for 32 years with the prestigious firm of Brown, Hahn, and Sanger. This group was very active in local and national politics, with Brown serving as postmaster general under Herbert Hoover and also chairing the Ohio Republican party and the National Republican party.

During the late 1920s Hahn was appointed to the bench as a federal district judge, and the firm changed its name to Brown and Sanger. Sanger was a very prominent attorney and was especially well known for his business and tax work. He died in 1946; it was at this time that Spengler and another attorney at the firm, Hebenstreit, went on to form Spengler Nathanson with their friends Joe Heyman and Joe Nathanson.

The first associate the firm took was Ben Durfee in 1948. It continued to grow, adding former city manager John McCarthy in 1956. Today it has 34 partners and associates with specializations in public law; labor law; business, which includes taxes and securities; litigation, which includes business and insurance defense; and estate planning and probate.

During the early years the firm specialized in public law, working with the University of Toledo, many high school and elementary school districts, and the Toledo Lucas County Port Author-

David A. Katz is the firm's managing partner.

ity. In fact the firm played a key role in the development of the Port Authority.

They were also instrumental in the formation of Food Town. Heyman says they became involved largely because of Joe Nathanson's reputation for fairness and ethics. "He brought together five people from independent groceries, and after a great deal of work and ingenuity, Food Town emerged."

Heyman credits Nathanson with infusing the firm with integ-

rity, a strong work ethic, and excellence in practice. "He was very thorough in everything he did—and in our business that can be critical. He and Bert Hebenstreit were two of the most brilliant and honorable men that I have ever met."

Spengler Nathanson has always had a strong public conscience, as evidenced by the number of members that have chosen to serve in public life and on numerous community boards and committees. "Otto Spengler was a very generous man," Heyman says, "and encouraged financial support for many worthy public institutions, and we've tried to continue that tradition throughout our history."

Spengler, Nathanson, Heyman, McCarthy & Durfee has been very active in the Toledo Bar Association through the years, with six of its members having served as president of the organization at one time or another. The members also have had three city law directors in their ranks and a former assistant U.S. attorney.

RIGHT: Ben Durfee (left) and Joe Heyman are named partners, of counsel.

BELOW: (From left) Jim Jensen (former assistant U.S. attorney) meets with management committee members B. Gary McBride, Frank T. Pizza (former city law director), David G. Wise, and Ted M. Rowen.

Heyman, who has been practicing law for 53 years, has seen many changes in the legal profession. Perhaps the most visible change has been growth—a growth he attributes to the many changes that have occurred in the social structure since the Roosevelt administration. "When I graduated from law school in 1937," he says, "new legislation was in process to try to correct social problems which were perceived to have caused the Depression. This resulted in a massive expansion of many fields of law such as labor, individual rights, and social responsibility. At that time there were between 500 and 600 lawyers in Toledo, a number that has grown to 2,000 today."

NFO Research, Inc.

Founded in 1946 by Howard A. Trumbull, a former general sales manager of the Libbey Glass Division of Owens-Illinois, NFO Research, Inc., is today widely recognized as one of the most experienced research firms in the United States and is a member of the Pergamon AGB plc group, an international conglomerate. Clients include all of the top consumer marketing companies in the country and are serviced by NFO offices in eight cities.

NFO strives to maintain industry leadership by providing creative solutions to even the toughest data gathering problems. The company offers a full line of marketing research services designed to meet clients' varied research needs.

Having pioneered panel research, NFO today maintains the largest consumer panel in America. The NFO Panel consists of more than 400,000 U.S. households, obtained through carefully developed recruiting methods, that have agreed to participate in research surveys. These 400,000 households represent one in every 226 households in the country—nearly one million individuals.

The NFO Panel contains the largest U.S. household sample available today that is balanced to national statistics. Constantly maintained within the panel are 40 individual groups of 5,000 households, each of which, through rigorous panel maintenance, is balanced to demographics from the latest available U.S Census Bureau statistics to be representative of the United States.

The representative portion of the panel is not only balanced to national statistics on age, income, market size, geographic region,

and household size, it also contains the proper proportion of family to nonfamily (single person) households and the proper proportion of households within each state and within the top metropolitan areas.

Extensive background information is collected and maintained for all panel households, making it possible for clients to select custom samples of respondents for marketing research studies at national, regional, and local market levels.

The NFO Panel offers efficiencies not available with other survey methods. Because panel members make the commitment early on to participate in surveys, response rates are high (as high as 70% to 80%) and survey questions are answered with both interest and honesty. Panelists complete surveys at home in comfortable, nonthreatening environments rather than at artificial test sites. Panelists are also usually willing to discuss personal or sensitive topics (i.e., finances, health issues). The Panel makes it easy to reach people who are typically difficult to locate through random sampling methods.

To ensure its effectiveness the NFO Panel is subjected to constant quality control measures. Addresses and telephone numbers of panelists are continuously updated. To prevent survey overuse of any households, NFO maintains strict use scheduling controls, and continuously freshens the representative portion of the panel with newly recruited households.

Depending upon a client's requirements, NFO can execute many types of research studies including in-home product testing; concept testing; attitude, awareness, and usage studies; advertising tracking surveys; owner/user

ABOVE: William E. Lipner, president and chief executive officer of NFO Research, Inc.

BELOW: NFO mails surveys and test products to consumers through its Toledo-based mail center, the largest single user of the Toledo Post Office and Toledo's United Parcel Service.

profiling; longitudinal studies; market segmentation studies; and studies using geo-demographic segmentation systems including PRIZM, ACORN, VISION, Cluster Plus, and the VALS 2 psychographic segmentation system.

NFO offers a complete range of telephone and mail data collection alternatives that make use of panel respondents, nonpanel random samples, or business respondents. NFO's Mail Center is the largest user of Toledo's Post Office and United Parcel Service. NFO handles between 275,000 and 300,000 pieces of incoming survey mail each month.

Telephone interviewing facilities are located in Toledo; Greensboro, North Carolina; and San

ABOVE: NFO's corporate headquarters is located at 2700 Oregon Road in Northwood.

RIGHT: NFO Research, Inc., completed over 500,000 telephone interviews nationwide last year.

Diego, California. Most interviewing stations are equipped with computer-assisted interviewing hardware making use of Bellview interviewing software, one of the most sophisticated interviewing softwares, known industrywide for its speed and accuracy. NFO completed more than 500,000 telephone interviews last year.

NFO's Multicard survey—a first of its kind omnibus mail survey—allows clients to share the cost of surveying large representative samples of U.S. households by combining their own noncompeting customized surveys into one mail packet. The Multicard, which mails twice each month, is widely used because of its economy.

The Multicard makes it possible to economically track changing behavior, attitudes, and trends over time. Companies can monitor changes in brand usage, brand awareness, and consumption volume, as well as establish scheduled observations of advertising effectiveness and consumer attitudes.

The Multicard enables marketers to screen large samples, as large as 150,000 panel households at once, for qualifying respondents

needed for follow-up studies. All survey results can be merged with household demographics to establish detailed customer profiles.

NFO prides itself on speedy data delivery once a survey is completed. A special service allows the delivery of final tabulated tables one business day after completion of phone work on telephone or combination mail/phone surveys. Another special service for mail panel surveys makes final tabulated reports available just 21 days after questionnaires are fielded, representing a 50 percent reduction of normal time requirements, while still obtaining NFO's normal return rates of 70 to 80 percent.

NFO has in-house data production capabilities that include coding, data entry, and data processing, with the latest DEC VAX computers. Special in-house software programs have been carefully designed to facilitate panel maintenance, data entry, verification, editing, sample selection, sample weighting, and preparation of NFO's highly sophisticated tabulation formats and calculations.

NFO has been quick to develop innovations to meet the emerging needs of the research industry. Its National Yellow Pages Monitor (NYPM) Division, based in San Francisco, operates a diary-based syndicated audience measurement rating service for Yellow Pages directories. NYPM was designed in response to the competitive environment created for Yellow Pages directories by the AT&T divestiture in 1984. Advertisers are now faced with decisions about which directory to advertise in. NYPM ratings are intended to

help them to make that decision.

Another recent introduction is SCREEN-TEST, a first of its kind video-based testing methodology. With over 70 percent of U.S. households owning VCRs, testing via videotape presentation is not only feasible, but very practical for many types of studies. Preidentified VCR-owning households are sent videotapes which demonstrate products, product ideas, or television commercials. Households review the tapes and react through mail or telephone surveys.

Hispanics currently make up eight percent of the U.S. population and are growing at a rate five times that of the non-Hispanic population. NFO has responded to marketers' growing needs to study this important consumer group with the opening of The Hispanic Research Center in San Diego and the introduction of The Hispanic Panel. The Hispanic Research Center, staffed with Spanish-speaking interviewers, provides a link to Hispanic consumers in major markets across the country, taking into account their unique cultural interests, diversities, and needs. The Hispanic Panel mirrors the NFO Panel in enabling clients to design custom research surveys among specially selected samples of Hispanics.

NFO Research, Inc., is a highly qualified, well-respected, and relied-on marketing research supplier providing marketers with expert guidance in designing, executing, and analyzing quality marketing research surveys.

The Schroeder Company

The Schroeder Company was founded by Edward Schroeder, Sr., in 1946 as a full-service land-development and property-management company with complete in-house facilities for land development, design, construction, marketing, and property management. During the past 44 years these groups have combined their talents to create apartment communities, suburban subdivisions, and mini-shopping centers of quality in northwestern Ohio and southeastern Michigan.

"Our primary goal is to provide clients with accurate and efficient development, design, and construction of their entire project," says Edward J. Schroeder, Jr., current president and son of the company's founder. Some of the developments in the Toledo area that Schroeder Company has been responsible for include McCord Woods Apartments, Riviera Apartments, Ravenswood Apartments, Byrneport Apartments, Norwich Apartments, Cambridge Court Apartments, Ottawa Cove Apartments, Fountain Square Apartments, and Byrneport Plaza. In addition, Schroeder Company owns and operates Westgate Storage, a mini-storage facility in the Westgate area.

Schroeder Company is currently constructing Country Club Apartments at Inverwest on Dorr Street. There will be a total of 316 luxury units.

The Schroeder company is also developing two subdivisions. One is Winding Brook, a southeastern Michigan subdivision off Smith Road between Jackman and Lewis avenues in Temperance, Michigan. The other is Riverford, located on Route 65, approximately two miles west of

Route 25 in Perrysburg. It is hoping to host the 1991 fall parade of homes in this conveniently located country setting. These new developments mark a return to single-family development by the Schroeder Company, which for the past decade has been concentrating on the development of apartment complexes and property management.

Edward Schroeder, Sr., was the first real estate developer in the area to build homes using FHA financing along with the initiation of 40-year mortgages. "My father always said success was a matter of timing and a sense of knowing how and when to do things," Schroeder says. "He once sold 70 homes in less than one hour—just by offering them for a $50 down payment and easy financing."

During the 1970s the company expanded to include construction of apartment complexes. Schroeder was the forerunner in the construction of low- to moderate-income multifamily communities. The company built, owns, and manages 1,300 apartment units. The property-management division also manages for other owners as well.

The Schroeder Company branched into commercial construction with the Byrneport Plaza, a six-bay shopping plaza, and Westgate Storage. Both were completed in 1987.

Recently Edward Schroeder III joined the company, heading the company's construction division, making the firm the second third-

ABOVE: Winding Brook in Temperance, Michigan, is one of two subdivisions developed by the Schroeder Company.

LEFT: The Schroeder Company built and manages McCord Woods Apartment Community in Toledo.

generation construction company in the Toledo area.

Edward Schroeder, Jr., feels the organization is unique because of the variety of disciplines it is involved in—construction, land development, and property management. The company has property-management assets in excess of $44 million and employs more than 60 people.

Schroeder has placed a great deal of emphasis on property management during the past decade. "We have carefully refined our management expertise to manage both our own property and others with profit productivity results. Clients who find self-management full of cost-prohibitive areas due to the extensive nature of property management can place their property in the capable hands of the our professional management team."

Photo by Jim Rohman

CHAPTER EIGHT

Quality
of Life

M edical, educational, and service institutions contribute to the quality of life of Toledo residents.

The University of Toledo, 106
Hospital Council of Northwest Ohio, 108
Envirosafe Services, Inc., 112
Consolidated Environmental Services, Inc., 113

Photo by Haz Keyser

The University of Toledo

Whenever anyone talks about Toledo's future growth, the University of Toledo's name is sure to be mentioned. That is because the university is an integral part of Toledo's future—providing tremendous people and facility resources to assist the business and nonprofit communities with redevelopment and growth.

The university is recognized as one of the fastest-growing research enterprises among Ohio's public colleges and universities. It is attracting millions of dollars from outside sources to fund research in virtually every part of the academic spectrum. And the results of this university-related research are quickly becoming a part of Toledo's economic livelihood.

One of the most visible projects in which the university assisted is the Edison Industrial Systems Center, which helps companies improve operations by combining engineering, business, and information systems technologies to achieve large-scale systems integration. Its goal is to keep Ohio industry competitive in global markets during the coming century. The university spearheaded the area effort to match a $4-million grant from Ohio's Thomas Edison Program to establish the center. Today the Edison Center has more than $10 million in funding.

Another significant university project is the Polymer Institute, which stemmed from a $500,000 donation of laboratory equipment and technical support from Owens Illinois Inc. The institute's mission is to research and develop ways to make stronger, lighter, and less expensive plastic—very important in Toledo because there are more than 100 companies in the area that manufacture industrial and consumer plastic products.

The university's Thin-Films Research Institute has more than $1 million in funding to develop advanced production techniques that could lower costs for thin-film solar cells and even make them feasible for utilities, satellite transmitters, and communications signals. Two area companies, Glasstech Inc. and Solar Cells Inc., have been instrumental in the development of this program along with the Ohio Department of Development and the university's physics and astronomy department.

The Eitel Institute for Silicates and Ceramics Research was established by the university in 1976. It received a big boost in March 1989, when Nippon Electric Glass Co. in Japan announced a $1.2-million gift to establish a fully endowed faculty chair in silicate science.

The university's Division of Business Research and Services has been involved with the Committee of 100 in establishing the Toledo/Lucas County Port Authority as the central agency for regional economic development. The Urban Affairs Center is part of the state's urban university program, working on preserving Toledo's neighborhoods through economic development, historic preservation, and grant applications. Researchers have also developed a computer model to help city officials project revenues from Toledo's payroll withholding tax.

Other University of Toledo projects are the Northwest Ohio Center for Labor-Management Cooperation, which investigates successful work environment and negotiating techniques. While it does not involve itself in mediation or arbitration, the center provides consultants, sets up conferences and workshops, and compiles research data to help improve labor relations. The Center for Drug Design and Development is one of the university's fastest-growing research centers, with work being conducted by the College of Pharmacy. Researchers and graduate students are looking at new drug treatments for neurological disorders and Alzheimer's Disease as well as at treatments that would avoid side effects found in some potent drugs.

One of the interesting aspects of all these research programs is that five years ago less than 5 percent of the funding was coming from the private sector. Today more than 30 percent comes from the private sector.

The University of Toledo has seen growth in enrollment as well as in the research dollars. Enrollment has increased 52 percent in the past 15 years with the total student population now exceeding 24,000 people. The university has also seen record increases in the

ABOVE: The University of Toledo's beautiful campus.

RIGHT: Faculty and students work together to promote excellence.

number of merit scholars among entering freshmen.

More than half of the student body comes from outside Lucas County and either directly or indirectly contributes more than $100 million annually to Toledo's economy.

The university has six baccalaureate colleges: arts and sciences; business administration; education and allied professions; law; engineering; pharmacy; and university college. There is also a College of Law. All now offer doctoral programs, except University College. Associate degree programs are also available through the university's Community and Technical College.

In all areas—research, facilities, and education—the University of Toledo strives to go beyond just being a school that serves a large population to a school that puts emphasis on excellence in every area of endeavor.

Hospital Council of Northwest Ohio

Flower Memorial Hospital

In 1910 Flower Memorial Hospital's predecessor opened in Toledo with a specific mission: "To maintain a general hospital for the care and treatment of the sick and injured with Christian solicitude."

While health care has changed dramatically, the hospital's mission has transcended the years. Flower Memorial Hospital is now a leading regional healthcare provider.

In 1975 Flower Memorial moved to Sylvania, Ohio, as part of the Flower Memorial Healthplex, which includes Lake Park Hospital and Nursing Center, a 250-bed extended-care/rehabilitation facility; and Crestview Club Apartments, a 150-unit luxury retirement center. With Flower Memorial Hospital's 300-bed capacity and state-of-the-art technology, the Healthplex offers quality care during a person's whole life. All three facilities benefit from their location near one another, as well as the beautiful 100-acre setting, sparkling with ponds and woods, yet just minutes from downtown Toledo.

The Healthplex features a variety of specialities and technological strengths, including magnetic resonance and CT imaging, lasers, family-centered maternity and pediatrics, rehabilitation center, cancer treatment, and special programs for health enhancement, diabetes, arthritis, and chemical dependency.

Medical College of Ohio

Fulfilling the vision its founders had almost 25 years ago, the Medical College of Ohio (MCO) and its three on-campus hospitals are making significant strides toward becoming one of the state's leading medical referral centers.

More than 50 percent of the approximately 7,000 patients admitted each year come from the 20 counties of northwestern Ohio. The Medical College Hospitals, the primary teaching institutions for MCO, include the 258-bed acute care hospital, the 36-bed Comprehensive Rehabilitation Hospital, and the 25-bed Child-Adolescent Psychiatric Hospital. An $11.3-million health center houses ambulatory clinics and faculty offices.

The hospitals draw on the expertise of more than 200 physicians who are also on faculty of the medical school. Among the services provided are open-heart surgery for children with congenital heart defects; heart, kidney, and cornea transplants; intraoperative radiation therapy for patients with certain types of cancer; hyperbaric oxygen therapy; comprehensive epilepsy services; and multidiscipli-

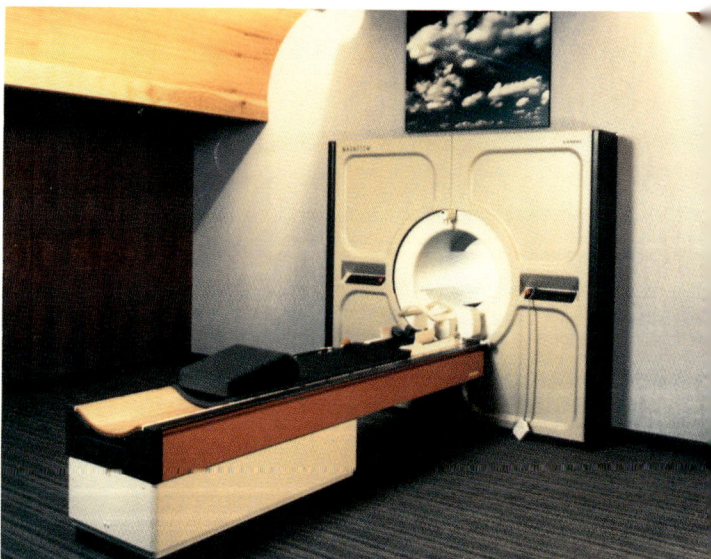

TOP: Flower Memorial Hospital

ABOVE: Flower Memorial's state-of-the-art technology helps to provide quality care throughout one's life.

nary cancer care.

Although many programs are for patients with complex medical problems, a variety of preventive medicine programs have been established to help patients adopt healthy life-styles and avoid serious illness and injuries.

Mercy Hospital of Toledo

Mercy Hospital, just off Interstate 75 near downtown Toledo, is a 294-bed facility with general and acute medical care and health care programs. Mercy is operated by the Sisters of Mercy, Cincinnati Province. Mercy's sister hospital is St. Charles Hospital in nearby Oregon, Ohio. Mercy Hospital presents a broad range of health care services. It demonstrates its tradition of excellence in the Endocrine and Diabetes Care Center, where a team of professionals coordinate their expertise to enable a person with diabetes to live a full and happy life.

Mercy's physician residency programs, including family practice, pathology, and transitional residencies, illustrate Mercy's dedication to nurturing the future of quality medical care providers. The Mercy School of Nursing provides a two-year diploma curriculum and a bachelor's degree program in conjunction with the Mercy College of Detroit.

Mercy continues its distinct heritage in a variety of other services and programs, including emergency services, adult intensive care units, mental health, neurology, diagnostic testing, and respiratory, physical, and occupational therapies. Mercy also serves the community through its various satellite locations for family practice, physical therapy, and laboratory services.

Mercy and St. Charles Hospitals together operate the Work Injury Network (WIN), a joint service providing employers with a dynamic range of industry-related health care services. Another joint service is Senior Advantage, offering older adults in the community a broad range of services, educational programs, and health screenings.

Parkview Hospital

Parkview Hospital is a 130-bed full-service, osteopathic medical center located at 1920 Parkwood Avenue, across the street from the Toledo Museum of Art. Parkview was founded in 1945 by a group of physicians dedicated to building a hospital that would be small and personal enough to attend to the special needs of every patient. Today Parkview has grown to be a progressive medical center that

BELOW: Parkview Hospital

BOTTOM: Riverside Hospital.

provides state-of-the-art treatment, while maintaining the personal environment philosophy upon which Parkview Hospital has grown throughout the years.

Parkview's more than 60 doctors of osteopathy (D.O.s) offer something special with explicit concern for their patient's environment, nutrition, and total well-being. Because D.O.s have a special understanding of the musculoskeletal system, they are able to determine how illness or injury will affect organs and systems in the body.

Hospital services include a general practice unit, progressive care unit, surgery, pediatrics, obstetrics, emergency department, and physical therapy. Parkview's physical therapy department provides treatment to assist in the recovery of surgery patients, injured workers, and athletes. Staffed by an outstanding team of physical therapists, orthopedic surgeons, physicians specializing in sports medicine, and exercise physiolo-

gists, Parkview Hospital's physical therapy department is among the best in the Toledo area.

"Best Personal Care" is the trademark that sets Parkview Hospital apart. With a focus on family health care and an emphasis on quality, the small and personal environment at Parkview offers area residents a unique choice in health care.

Riverside Hospital

As a leader in the areas of obstetrical care, wellness, prevention, and outpatient surgery, Riverside Hospital is the choice health care provider for residents of northwest Ohio and southeast Michigan.

Starting in 1883 solely as a maternal care facility, Riverside Hospital, a 271-bed community hospital near downtown Toledo, is the flagship of the Riverside Health Group—a corporate entity that provides a wide range of services to the community through all its members. Riverside offers close, personal attention, efficient deliv-

ery of health care, and a strong partnership with its medical staff.

Along with quality inpatient care, Riverside offers the latest in outpatient care through Health-Mark Pavilion, a leader in outpatient surgery and services. Subsidiaries of Riverside Health Group include two urgent care centers servicing east and south Toledo; HealthEquip, a durable medical equipment company; and Partners in Home Care, a home health and wellness center with programs ranging from health education, physical fitness, sports medicine, back care, behavioral medicine, and weight management.

St. Charles Hospital

St. Charles Hospital is a 342-bed community hospital conveniently located just off Interstate 280 at the corner of Navarre Avenue (Route 2) and Wheeling Street in Oregon.

A sister hospital to Mercy Hospital of Toledo operated by the Sisters of Mercy, Cincinnati Province, St. Charles Hospital has developed a host of innovative health care programs, such as the advanced psychiatric care unit and the Talbot Outpatient Center for people with substance abuse problems. The Pain Management Center, the first chronic-pain clinic of its kind in northwest Ohio, offers an intensive, outpatient therapy program to treat those with debilitating pain.

St. Charles Hospital also provides a full range of health care services featuring the newest in medical technology, including surgery, an emergency center, special care nursery for high-risk newborns, adult intensive care units, pediatrics, a rehabilitation center

The Toledo Hospital

adjacent to the main campus, oncology, and other diagnostic and treatment services. St. Charles Hospital is an innovative leader in the health care field.

St. Luke's Hospital
St. Luke's Hospital is a modern health care facility conveniently located in Maumee, Ohio, at the intersection of Interstate 475 and the Anthony Wayne Trail. Although St. Luke's has inpatient services for medical/surgical, pediatric, intensive, coronary, and emergency care, only one in seven of its patients actually stays overnight. The others take advantage of a wide variety of services, including outpatient diagnostic, therapeutic, surgical, and preventive care.

Special programs have also been designed to meet special needs. This include Mend 'n Tend, which offers day care for sick children, and SeniorService, a comprehensive program for those 55 years of age and older.

St. Luke's has services usually associated with major medical centers such as urodynamics and endurology, microscopic, endoscopic and laser surgery, orthopedic joint replacement, CT scanning, and nu-

clear medicine. Outpatient rehabilitation and counseling programs in cardiology, diabetes control, pulmonary medicine, nutrition, and physical therapy are also available.

St. Luke's Hospital is big enough to offer all the advantages of modern medical technology, yet small enough to give the type of care that cannot be put into prescription bottles.

St. Vincent Medical Center
St. Vincent Medical Center is a leading tertiary care and referral center for a tri-state region, with patients coming from more than 20 counties in Ohio, Michigan, and Indiana.

Founded by the Grey Nuns of Montreal in 1855 as Toledo's first hospital, St. Vincent has grown to 642 beds and encompasses resources that are the hallmarks of a major medical center. The medical staff of more than 600 physicians represents more than 50 medical and surgical specialties.

Leading the region in surgery technology, St. Vincent has continually provided pacesetting health care. Among its distinctive services are Life Flight, the Regional Burn Care and Reconstructive Center, the Northwest Ohio Heart Center, Tennyson Center for chemical dependency treat ment, and a

progressive obstetrics program that introduced the area's first birthing centers.

The St. Vincent School of Nursing was the first hospital-based Catholic school of nursing in the State of Ohio and offers a three-year diploma program.

The Toledo Hospital
Staffed with skilled, caring professionals from a wide range of disciplines and equipped with some of the most sophisticated equipment available, The Toledo Hospital delivers quality care in the comfortable surroundings of a modern medical center.

Established in 1874, the hospital is now the largest medical institution and referral center in northwest Ohio. As a recognized leader in health care delivery within the Great Lakes region, the hospital ranks as one of the most progressive medical centers in the United States. Several of its specialized services have been developed into comprehensive centers of excellence, such as The Reuben Center for Women and Children, offering concentrated treatment and therapy.

A nonprofit institution, The Toledo Hospital is an affiliate of ProMedica Health Systems Inc., its parent holding company. ProMedica Health Systems also includes several subsidiaries, among them Caring Services, a home health care agency, and medical office buildings. In addition, the hospital belongs to a network of some of the nation's most prestigious hospitals through its membership as a shareholder in the Voluntary Hospitals of America, Inc.

Envirosafe Services, Inc.

Envirosafe Services, Inc., (ESI) provides waste management services for a wide variety of government agencies, municipalities, and businesses throughout the United States. Envirosafe maintains corporate headquarters near Valley Forge, Pennsylvania. The company has two major hazardous-waste disposal sites: one in northwestern Ohio near Toledo and the other in Idaho. It also has two proposed disposal facilities in Pennsylvania and Texas as well as field service and regional sales offices nationwide.

Envirosafe is proud of its Environmental Protection compliance record and considers itself a true environmentalist. Its management maintains that "philosophically, we should be able to recycle everything." The firm believes society is working toward this goal but realistically is a long way from it. In the meantime there needs to be a

safe, contained place to store waste products, and that is where Envirosafe comes in.

Envirosafe Services, Inc., (ESI) has been a pioneer in developing appropriate waste management systems and is one of the principal companies of its kind in the country. Its operations are staffed by experts in the analysis, testing, handling, and disposal of hazardous and nonhazardous materials. They provide needed waste management services for companies in many fields, from agriculture to automotive and from pharmaceutical to petrochemical.

The Ohio facility receives materials from customers primarily located throughout the East and Midwest. Once materials reach the facility, they are tested, handled in an approved fashion, and stored in disposal cells that are sealed with specially designed polyethylene liners. The cells are surrounded by natural deposits of extremely dense clays that add further protection. Sophisticated

air, soil, and water testing is carried on continuously to ensure maximum protection of the environment.

As America's commitment to a clean environment has grown, it has become increasingly apparent that thousands of sites nationwide suffer from the ravages of improper waste disposal practices. Envirosafe has been an important factor in the cleanup of these sites for years through its ACES unit, a well-regarded organization that celebrates its 28th anniversary in 1990. ACES, which has been an important remediation company in the northeastern United States specializing in hazardous-waste site cleanup, facility decontamination, and tank cleaning, was recently sold by ESI. This move primarily signals ESI's commitment to focus on being the nation's premeir industrial/hazardous treatment and disposal facility.

Each year Americans demand more from their government to ensure the protection of the environment for future generations. And each year more and more American businesses commit themselves to scientifically correct management of wastes that are the inevitable result of manufacturing processes. The ultimate success of such efforts to protect the environment requires that government and industry collaborate effectively with waste management companies that are able to assume the the responsibility for many types of wastes.

Envirosafe Services, Inc., believes in helping to protect the environment by using the most sophisticated technology available to ensure that these industrial/hazardous wastes are safely disposed of.

Envirosafe's Ohio facility.

Consolidated Environmental Services, Inc.

Consolidated Environmental Services, Inc. (CES), prides itself on being an organization that not only cares about the environment but does something about it. From taking care of an asbestos problem in a local school to cleaning up an oil spill in a nearby creek, CES helps to maintain a safe environment in the Toledo area.

Dennis A. Siefke, an expert in hazardous-waste management, formed CES because of the growing need for environmental services and the increased number of regulations imposed by the Environmental Protection Agency. "The staggering environmental problems facing our world today are of increasing concern as we move into the future," says Siefke. "Because of advanced research and environmental testing, we are continually learning what needs to be done to protect our environment's future."

With a long list of environmental services, CES specializes in emergency-response cleanups and asbestos abatement. It also has extensive experience in hazardous/nonhazardous waste-site remediation; tank cleaning, removal, and installation; PCB cleanups; contaminated soil excavation; wastewater treatment; and pond sludge removal.

CES services commercial, governmental, and industrial clients in Ohio and surrounding states. Emergency-response service is provided within a 300 mile radius of Toledo. An example of CES' experience is the one-half mile cleanup of Duck Creek in Toledo. CES contained, cleaned, and disposed of the lime sludge that was in the creek as a result of a leak in a water processing plant due to vandalism.

CES also removed and disposed of 6,000 square feet of cyanide-containing concrete from a local manufacturing plant and removed 32,000 square feet of asbestos-containing material in an area school.

Currently CES employs approximately 125 full-time people and has a staff of managers with more than 100 combined years of experience in the hazardous-waste field.

Hazardous-material handling requires special skills and experience as well as ongoing education. CES field personnel receive regular comprehensive training in addition to federally mandated 40-hour training.

"Through our commitment to excellence and service CES plays a vital role in the field of environmen-

Consolidated Environmental Services, Inc., does its part to make Toledo a safe and beautiful place to live.

tal research and restoration," Siefke says. CES pledges that it will continue to be active in review, assessment, and research of new techniques for environmental management.

CHAPTER NINE

Marketplace

Toledo's retail establishments and accommodations are enjoyed by residents and visitors.

The Toledo Marriott, 116
Seaway Food Town, 118
Toledo Hilton, 120

Photo by Ann Winder

114

The Toledo Marriott

The Toledo Marriott is beautifully situated on the Maumee River in the heart of the city's business and financial district. It is convenient to the Seagate Convention Centre and downtown corporate offices via climate-controlled walkways.

As Toledo's only four-diamond hotel, the Marriott's management staff sets high standards for quality and service. They pride themselves on their ability to tune in to client needs, whether it's complicated arrangements for a large convention or a husband and wife seeking a pleasurable getaway weekend. The goal of everyone, from the valet parking a car to the receptionist, is to provide each guest with a memorable hotel experience.

All rooms at the Marriott feature individual climate control, a color TV with remote control, free cable service, in-room pay movies, an alarm clock, an AM/FM radio, and a telephone with a message light. Non-smoking and wheelchair-accessible rooms are available. The luxury hotel has 245 guest rooms and suites as well as one permanent board room which can accommodate 12 people.

The Marriott also offers a full complement of guest services, including a gift shop, valet service, room service, beverage machines, free ice, office services, and more. Adjacent to the hotel in an underground mall is a travel agency, a rental car desk, a barber shop, a bank, and a pharmacy.

Excellence in dining and entertainment is also a trademark of the Marriott. Ashley's elegant ambiance overlooking the Maumee River makes it the preferred choice for important business meals and social occasions. The

The Toledo Marriott is beautifully situated on the Maumee River in the heart of the city's business and financial district.

Regatta Bar & Grill, also overlooking the river, offers dining in casual comfort featuring fresh seafood and pasta.

An Executive Health Club is available, and boating, sailing, golf, tennis, and fishing are nearby. The hotel is also adjacent to an outdoor ice-skating rink for those who like exercise on crisp winter days.

If you are organizing an important business meeting, or hosting a very special social event, the Marriott's function and banquet facilities are designed to accommodate your needs. The hotel boasts more than 14,000 square feet of newly renovated, professionally designed, and exceptionally versatile meeting, banquet, and exhibition space.

Highlighting this space is the Grand Ballroom with its 14 foot high ceilings. This room can accommodate 850 for dinner or can be divided into six sections for smaller groups. There are also six additional meeting rooms, located directly across an expansive prefunction corridor. Two handsomely appointed hospitality suites are also available for smaller higher-level business meeting or social functions.

The Marriott's award-winning catering professionals are known for their special touches—the creative canapes, the folded linen napkins, the sumptuous spread of decorative desserts. Unbounded imagination, the freshest ingredients, and expert food preparation will give an affair that extra flair.

Whether a breakfast business

meeting, a casual luncheon, or an extravagant evening reception, a menu can be designed that fits every mood.

Choose from a diverse selection of chef's specialities, prepared with the utmost care for the most discriminating tastes. Oven-fresh pastries, pineapple boats, and finger foods tempt the most discriminating palate.

Fresh cut vegetables, vine-ripened fruit, creative sauces, and savory seasonings round out the choices for exceptional cuisine. An

enticing selection of aromatic coffees, bubbling beverages, and vintage wines complement the menu for a most pleasing experience.

The Marriott is especially proud of the work they have done with non-profit groups to make their events really special and profitable. They have been home to such premier events as the Sapphire Ball and The Ability Center's Fall Fashion Preview.

The Toledo Marriott is owned and operated by Interstate Hotels Corporation. Interstate is the largest franchisee in the Marriott system and is one of the nation's fastest-growing hospitality companies. Corporate objectives include rapid, but carefully planned, growth; consistent quality of existing and new assets; high levels of profitability; and attraction, development, and retention of an experienced and highly competent management team.

Interstate has a firm commitment to achieving the highest possible quality in all aspects of the hospitality business. It recognizes the necessity for continuing superior performance in all areas and is committed to enduring excellence. The company has just completed a $500 million renovation of the Toledo Marriott lobby, business and meeting rooms. Everything is now done in understated mauve and green tones. Renovation of the guest rooms will start in the near future. Marriott is committed to Toledo and its future and intends to continue its tradition of being the finest hotel in the area.

Seaway Food Town

Chairman of the Board and Chief Executive Officer Wallace D. Iott has led Seaway Food Town, Inc., from its pre-World War II beginnings as a neighborhood grocery at Wernert's Corners, to Wally's Food Town in 1946, to a major force in the grocery industry with sales exceeding one-half billion dollars.

Today the Seaway Food Town organization includes such well-known companies as Balduf Bakery, Toledo Milk Processing, Valley Farm Foods, Kash 'n' Karry, Buck-

The Food Town Plus store concept has grown in acceptance and popularity since the first one opened in 1988

eye Specialties, the Pharm Deep Discount Drug Stores, and Food Town Plus, a combination store featuring a pharmacy, video rental, non-food items, service meat and fresh seafood, full service floral shops, a snack bar, a take-out deli, one-hour photofinishing, UPS shipping, a salad bar, and many other customer conveniences.

Jeanette Iott kept the family grocery store going during World War II while her husband was in the service. After the war, Wally Iott returned and invested his savings in Wally's Food Town, a

7,500-square-foot supermarket across the street from his original store.

In 1948 Iott and five other independent northwest Ohio grocers, Paul Pope, Frank Ulrich, Tom Swinghammer, Joe Altschuler, and Oscar Joseph, formed a buying and advertising co-op using the name Food Town. They had six stores among them.

Nine years later the co-op became incorporated under the name Seaway Food Town, Inc. Wally Iott was elected president and chairman. The first year's

sales were $15,800,000—less than two weeks' sales today. The first corporate store opened in Findlay, Ohio.

In 1959 the new company acquired West Toledo Wholesale Produce Distributors and became its own produce supplier. Growth continued, and three years later Seaway Food Town joined Staff Supermarket Associates, a private label buying co-op of other small, regional chains and introduced the Staff brand to its customers.

In 1962 Seaway Food Town had its first public offering of 125,000 shares of stock. That same year the company opened store #17 in Toledo. It incorporated an extensive non-foods department serviced by Ben Franklin, Inc. This was unprecedented in the industry at the time and set a trend for the future.

The next year proved just as busy for Seaway Food Town as they moved their corporate offices and warehouse from a vacant storefront in Toledo to a former cabinet factory in Maumee, Ohio. They

also acquired four stores from National Tea in Toledo when that company exited the market. This brought Seaway Food Town's total number of stores to 23.

The company entered the wholesale food service business in 1966 by acquiring Portion Control Meats, Inc. That same year they joined together with Driggs Dairy to form Toledo Milk Processing, Inc., a full line processor of milk products.

Two years later they further expanded the food business by acquiring Vlasic Foods of Ohio and Snow Maid Frozen Food, Inc. To better manage all the various food service operations they had acquired, the Company merged all of the food service into a single unit called Valley Farm Foods. In addition to servicing its own grocery stores, Valley Farm also distributed perishables to their own food stores and other food retailers in the northwestern Ohio market area.

Seaway Food Town introduced the warehouse market concept to Toledo with the opening of its first Kash 'n' Karry Warehouse Market in 1976.

The company continued to add to its traditional grocery stores with the acquisition of six Joseph's Supermarkets in Toledo; six Fisher Foods stores in Columbus; and

ABOVE: The Food Town Holiday Parade rings in the season for children of all ages.

BELOW: Food Town's successful Apples for the Students Program has allowed many schools to develop their computer labs with free Apple equipment

ten T&A Supermarkets in north central Ohio.

Seaway branched out into the drug store business in 1986 by converting a former supermarket in Findlay to a W.D.'s Deep Discount store. They then acquired the Pharm Deep Discount Drugstores in Toledo.

The company opened its first Food Town Plus in Tiffin, Ohio, in 1988. The Plus stores are Seaway's newest generation of combination stores, ranging in size from 48,000 to 60,000 square feet. This concept was very well accepted by consumers, and several Plus stores have now been added in the Toledo market.

Seaway Food Town has long been a leader in the employee services field with sponsorship of athletic activities, including an employee picnic and softball tournament, a blood drive, a savings bond program, scholarships, a safety poster contest for employees' children, participation in Walk America, and a bagging contest with awards.

Food Town also believes strongly in community involvement,

and its civic commitments include many non-profit organizations, such as Easter Seals, the Arthritis Foundation, Children's Miracle Network, and March of Dimes.

Two areas of prime interest to Food Town are education and arts and entertainment. The company began the Apples for the Students Program to award computers to schools who have saved register tapes. This year over 800 schools have signed up to participate. During 1989 $1.3 million in Apple Computer equipment and software was placed, at no cost, in more than 520 area schools.

In the arts, Food Town is the major underwriter of the Opera's Broadway Season and The Toledo Repertoire's 1990-1991 season. The company believes both programs offer customers a chance to enjoy quality entertainment at reduced rates while giving Toledo a chance to benefit from great theater.

Other projects include work with The Toledo Museum of Art and the Toledo Zoo. Food Town was a major sponsor of both the Panda and the Dinosaurs Alive exhibits.

Food Town is also in the process of revitalizing the Toledo Christmas Parade. The company is committed to returning it as the major event it was 20 years ago. To insure the parade's success, Food Town is both funding and maintaining a hands-on approach to making the dream a reality.

Through all these projects Food Town continually proves its dedication and support of its home town.

Toledo Hilton

While many hotels offer meeting and conference facilities, the Toledo Hilton offers them on a scale found only at the nation's largest hotels. The Hilton boasts the area's most complete meeting and banquet facilities. According to the management, the Hilton is the one hotel in Toledo that has everything—from a complete fitness center to luxurious rooms to delicious dining.

The Eleanor N. Dana Conference Center that is connected to the Toledo Hilton features 17 meeting rooms encompassing more than 13,000 square feet and has the latest in audiovisual equipment. In addition, the Hilton's 4,638-square-foot ballroom can accommodate groups as large as 400. The room can also be divided into six smaller rooms that can host groups from 36 to 110 people.

To unwind after meetings are finished, guests may use the hotel's fully equipped health and fitness center. The Morse Fitness Center features an indoor track, exercise equipment, and basketball and racquetball courts. The center is accessible via an interior walkway from the hotel. Guests may also relax in the indoor pool, spa, or sauna.

The Hilton is also very proud of its staff. "The best facilities in the world are useless if they don't come with a professional staff," says the Hilton's general manager. That is why the staff at the Hilton follows the simple philosophy,

"You take all the credit, we do the work."

Every planner on the staff is a stickler for detail. They are trained to pay attention to the smallest detail. With this expertise and experience they strive to anticipate guests' needs and wants. Whether someone is planning a rehearsal dinner, a major conference, wedding reception, or a highly technical audiovisual presentation, the staff has what it takes to make the event a success.

Located on the 350-acre park-like campus of the Medical College of Ohio, the Toledo Hilton features 213 luxurious guests rooms with color television, generous closet space, and a large work area including a desk and telephone. And because of its central location, guests are just minutes from the area's varied attractions, such as the Toledo Zoo, the Toledo Art Museum, and the Portside Fes-

The Toledo Hilton has everything to make a guest's stay a special experience.

tival Marketplace.

Excellent catering is another asset at the Hilton. The staff can satisfy a group's every whim with meals, snacks, and hors d'oeuvres served in the finest Hilton style. From a hot and hearty breakfast to haute cuisine, the Toledo Hilton can meet every guest's culinary needs and cravings. When not dining with a group, guests can feast in the hotel's highly acclaimed Iris Restaurant, which is open daily from 7 A.M. until 10 P.M.. Room service is also available from early morning until 10 P.M.

With luxurious guests rooms, fine dining, a fitness center that rivals the finest private clubs, a state-of-the-art conference center, and a hospitable staff, the Toledo Hilton has everything to make a guest's stay a special experience.

Photo by Haz Keyser

CHAPTER TEN

Manufacturing

Producing and distributing goods for individuals and industry, manufacturing firms provide employment for Toledo area residents.

Dana Corporation, 124
Owens-Corning Fiberglas, 126
Hydra-matic Division, 127
Glasstech, Inc., 128
Libbey-Owens-Ford Co., 130
The Kroger Company, 132
TL Industries, Inc., 134
Sun Oil Company, 135

Photo by Sue Keyser

Dana Corporation

Dana Corporation is one of the 100 largest industrial corporations in the United States and one of the 250 largest in the world. More than 38,000 Dana employees work in almost 700 facilities in 25 different countries. The company is a global leader in the manufacturing and marketing of systems, products, and services for the vehicular and industrial original equipment and replacement markets.

Dana began in 1904 as Spicer Manufacturing. The company's founder, Clarence Spicer, patented the first practical automotive drive shaft, replacing the chain-and-sprocket drive system then in use. In 1914 Charles A. Dana, a lawyer, politician, and businessman, took over as head of Spicer Manufacturing to provide financial and management guidance. In recognition of his contributions, Spicer Manufacturing was renamed Dana Corporation in 1946. Sales first passed $100 million in 1945 and one billion dollars in 1974; sales reached $5 billion in 1989. In the last 10 years alone, sales and profits have both tripled as Dana has expanded worldwide in five major markets and diversified for financial strength.

Through more than 80 years of doing business, Dana has maintained a commitment to excellence. To customers that commitment means leadership in quality, technology, and cost effectiveness. To shareholders it means continuously increasing the value of their Dana investment, symbolized by more than 200 consecutive dividends and the record of having never recorded an annual loss. To Dana

ABOVE: Charles A. Dana, shown here with Dana workers in 1934, knew the value of advice which was "direct from the workman. "He closely monitored the opinions of his employees throughout his 52-year leadership of Dana Corporation.

BELOW: Today, Dana's chairman and chief executive officer, Southwood J. "Woody" Morcott (right), continues the practice of seeking the advice of Dana people. Here, he consults with a worker while on a tour of one facility of Dana's Engine Products Division in Richmond, Indiana.

employees it means encouraging individual participation and initiative through the Dana style of management.

Dana's competitive success combines with wide recognition as one of the best managed companies based in the United States. The company's management philos-

ophy, the "Dana Style," emphasizes self-management and on-the-job involvement of all Dana people. The "Dana Style" emphasizes participation, communication, and identity with the company through such tactics as: productivity gain sharing plans, promotion from within, ownership of the company through an employee stock-purchase plan, and continuous training and education.

Dana recognizes the contribution of Dana people in its company strategy statement by challenging them to "Grow better as we grow bigger" and to "Grow with what we know and build on our strengths."

Dana's continuous improvement strategy requires setting a goal and measuring daily progress toward it in small but visible steps. "Our goal is to achieve our purpose as a company—earn money for our shareholders and increase the value of their investment," says Southwood "Woody" Morcott, chairman and chief executive officer. "A good measure of our progress is to assess Dana's annual improvement in three basic areas: strategy, shown by growth in distribution; operations, seen in the excellence programs for manufacturing and distribution; and style, evident in the involvement

improve operations in each facility, involvement furthered by strong emphasis on education.

Morcott boasts proudly that Dana people have saved millions of dollars with improvement ideas and suggestions, enhanced by innovative training programs. Involvement and education enable Dana people to improve daily profitability and performance.

Every Dana person has the responsibility and commitment to maintain the highest competitive standards. As Charles A. Dana said more than a half-century ago, "The one thing really worthwhile about an organization is its men and women. Stone and mortar, bricks and machinery can be duplicated, but the workers cannot." According to Morcott, Dana people have been a reflection of that belief since the company was started in 1904.

Throughout the years Dana Corporation has also exhibited a strong commitment to communities in which it does business. Each year the Dana Foundation contributes to a wide variety of activities from United Way to school programs to concerts and museums. "We also encourage volunteer participation by all Dana people," Morcott adds. "We're very excited about an experimental program we're underwriting for Toledo Public Schools wherein they try to identify children at risk at earlier ages than ever before. Then they work with them on self-esteem. If they're successful, the impact on a community could be tremendous."

TOP: The distribution of repair and replacement parts is an important and growing area of business for Dana. This facility in Milton-Keynes, England, is one of a network of 300 distribution centers worldwide.

ABOVE: Dana provides its employees with the opportunity to take advantage of 250,000 hours of training each year. Here, instructor Sue Kincade conducts a class at Dana University, located adjacent to corporate headquarters in Toledo.

and training of Dana people."

Distribution is of strategic importance to Dana because of its market size, profitability, and steady, non-cylindrical growth. The company's overall objective for its distribution market is to grow at twice the market rate, targeting combined distribution at 50 percent of total sales. Dana's successes in the distribution areas have caused distribution sales to grow almost four times faster than total sales in the past 20 years.

Continuous improvement in Dana operations drives the excellence in manufacturing and distribution programs and the company's regional assembly and global supply activities. "Our goal is to steadily reduce waste and to use our assets more effectively," Morcott says.

In 1989 this helped to reduce Dana's inventory to sales ratio, increase sales per person, and further expand the 70-plus quality awards from major customers. Through 1989 Dana employees had more than 270,000 hours of "excellence" training. Continuous operations improvement makes Dana a tough global competitor for market opportunities. According to Morcott, the excellence programs and global asset base "will continue to focus on providing the highest return on shareholders' investment."

Continuous improvement typifies the "Dana Style," making Dana people the production force behind the company's growth. During the past several years this style has created continuous improvement by stressing individual involvement to

Owens-Corning Fiberglas

Owens-Corning Fiberglas occupies the number one position in every major market it serves. It is known to the general public primarily for its familiar pink insulation and its roofing products. Founded more than 50 years ago, Owens-Corning is the world's leading manufacturer of fiberglass products and reinforcement materials and a major producer of polyester resins, with operations in more than two dozen countries worldwide.

Fiberglass products are used in all types of construction, as well as for more diverse applications—from glass fiber reinforcements for auto

parts to multilayered printed circuit boards for personal computers.

Owens-Corning got its start in the early 1930s, when researchers from Owens-Illinois and Corning Glass Works combined their efforts to see if glass fibers could be produced commercially and to find viable markets for a joint manufacturing and marketing venture. Since then the products and the company have carved a significant place in the annals of business. The firm is a New York Stock Exchange listed company, an international Fortune 500 company, and an employer of more than 18,000 people.

Owens-Corning is organized

into two major operating segments. The Industrial Materials Group manufactures and distributes glass fibers in a variety of forms worldwide. In addition, the group produces polyester resins used in the production of fiberglass reinforced plastics. These materials are sold to fabricators whose products include jet aircraft, home appliances, heavy equipment, automobiles, recreational equipment, road signs, sailing and power boats, textiles, and chemical pipe.

The second Owens-Corning operating segment is the Construction Products Group. It manufactures and distributes insulation and roofing products for new residential and commercial construction, home repair and remodeling, commercial renovation, manufactured housing, and appliance manufacturing.

As the largest manufacturer of residential insulation and roofing shingles, Owens-Corning has the highest consumer brand recognition in the industry with its use of the animated Pink Panther™ in its advertisements.

In addition to supplying insulation to new construction markets, replacement roofing offers opportunity for future growth as the large number of homes constructed during the 1950s and 1960s require roof replacement. U.S. Department of Energy recommendations for increased attic insulation in existing homes should also spur reinsulation demand.

Owens-Corning manufactures

ABOVE: The company uses glass fibers to make a variety of materials including those used in jet aircraft, home appliances, automobiles, recreational equipment, and textiles.

LEFT: Owens-Corning Fiberglas is known all over the world for its familiar pink insulation products.

and sells its products through an international network of subsidiaries, affiliates, and licensees. The firm has been particularly successful in Europe and has recently entered into new licensing agreements in Taiwan, Korea, and India. In 1989 the firm purchased its remaining ownership interest in its major Canadian affiliate, Fiberglas Canada Inc., one of the leading industrial concerns in that country.

Owens-Corning projects a bright future. There is a growing world demand for fiberglass products. The firm maintains a strong annual investment in research and development. Innovative processes and manufacturing improvements continue to contribute to the company's overall operating efficiency. New products, including a line of insulated fiberglass window frames and a laminated, fungus-resistant shingle, have been developed, tested, and introduced.

Owens-Corning Fiberglas is a company committed to building on its heritage—an ongoing search for new product applications for its fiberglass manufacturing and marketing expertise.

Hydra-matic Division

At first glance it looks like any other automobile component manufacturing facility in the United States. Like most plants it is large and located off of a busy thoroughfare. Its facade is fronted by neatly trimmed bushes and well-kept flower gardens. Inside, the similarities continue. Skilled hands manipulate massive machines while forklift drivers haul parts past employees intent on keeping the product rolling down the assembly line.

The Hydra-matic Division's Toledo plant is similar to other plants aesthetically, but there the commonality ends. What is not seen is the action behind the scenes and on the assembly line. The trained eye will recognize involved workers, high productivity, and a product quality rating among the best in the world. The result is over 1.7 million transmissions produced each year; a world-competitive product in cost, quality, and durability; and a nationally recognized employee involvement program.

Hydra-matic Toledo and UAW Local 14 is a partnership that is credited with making this General Motors facility a very successful operation in an industry once noted more for its adversarial relationships than partnerships. Today, the partnership is in full bloom at the Alexis Road plant.

The key is employee involvement. From their first day, employees have the opportunity to be involved in groups that influence decisions on health and safety, quality control, employee communication, education and training, ergonomics, and employee attendance. The Education and Training department is a state leader in providing adult and continuing education opportunities for employees. Employee Involvement groups, where hourly and salaried employees work together, have been credited with finding solutions saving the plant millions of dollars. Employees trained in resolving ergonomic concerns meet with the workers to redesign jobs. And work teams regularly meet with customers and vendors to determine product concerns and seek solutions.

Hydra-matic hourly employees are represented by the United Automobile, Aerospace, and Agricultural Implement Workers of America, Local No. 14. UAW Local 14 is rich in history and is distinguished as one of the earliest local unions established in the international workers' union.

Throughout its history the Toledo plant operations have been directed toward General Motors' passenger car and light-duty truck applications. The plant currently produces the Hydra-matic 4L60 4-speed automatic overdrive rear-wheel transmission. The unit is featured in Chevrolet and GMC light-duty trucks, vans, and utility vehicles; Chevrolet Camaro, Caprice, and Corvette; Pontiac Firebird; and Holden's (Australia) Commodore.

ABOVE: Hydra-matic Division's Toledo plant produces over 1.7 million high-quality transmissions each year.

BELOW: Personnel throughout the plant regularly schedule employee involvement meetings to resolve various issues, including those relating to the work environment, quality, cost considerations, and communication among work groups.

Glasstech, Inc.

Like St. Matthew's biblical reference about the prophet who is without honor in his own land, Perrysburg's Glasstech, Inc., may be better known around the world than in its home area. Founded in 1971 by Harold A. McMaster and Norman C. Nitschke (two former Libbey-Owens-Ford Glass Co. employees) and Frank A. Larimer, Glasstech is now the country's leading manufacturer of glass tempering and bending equipment. Glasstech manufactured equipment produces about 50 percent of the world's market share of tempered glass in the automotive and architectural industries.

The Perrysburg-based company's sales have risen from $2.6 million in 1976 to more than $90 million in 1989. This represents a compounded annual growth rate of 32 percent.

Michael J. Cicak, Glasstech's president since 1983, credits this growth to innovation with an emphasis on engineering, creativity, and inventing. The company devotes a level of resources to research and development that is unequaled in the world glass bending and tempering industry. Approximately one-third of Glasstech's employees are involved in research and development, and most of them are scientists and engineers with advanced degrees. Because of this emphasis the company holds more than 350 patents worldwide.

To meet the design demands of the 1990s, Glasstech introduced the Advanced Windshield Forming System for the automotive glass market and the Advanced Bending and Tempering System for Architectural Glass.

Looking at tomorrow's designs for automobiles, one can

ABOVE: Glasstech's Perrysburg complex includes a 220,000-square-foot corporate headquarters and a 96,000-square-foot research facility.

BELOW: Harold A. McMaster, company chairman and chief executive officer.

see that designers are using more and more glass. Designers already knew that Glasstech's Deep Bend system formed back-lites and sidelites with curves and bends that produce a total, wraparound look. It is a natural progression for designers to begin incorporating frontal-glass treatments, featuring inverse curves that gracefully blend windshields into roof and hood lines while wrapping even further around the sides. Glasstech's Advanced Windshield Forming System makes that possible.

In the architectural area Glasstech's advanced system now makes

it possible to bend and temper architectural glass in sizes up to 84 inches wide and 144 inches long in one, quick, continuous process. This horizontal system shapes glass of varying thicknesses into graceful, custom-specified curves with contours ranging from flat to a minimum radius of 20 inches. The result of this new innovation should be the additional use of high-quality, curved architectural glass for building facades, architectural landscaping, work stations, balustrades, shower enclosures, and even furniture.

The driving force behind these developments, as he has been with all of Glasstech's technological innovations to date, is McMaster. During his more than 50-year career, McMaster's name has been listed as principal inventor on more than 80 U.S. patents and as co-inventor on countless additional patents.

An unassuming individual, McMaster has an inquisitive and innovative mind that is forever probing and questioning. While his developments have dealt primarily with glass bending and tempering, his interests are much broader. For example, during the energy crunch of the early 1970s, he began to seriously consider the future of solar energy. As a result, McMaster, personally, and Glasstech, as a corporation, have become involved financially in the formation of two additional companies involved in commercializing solar energy.

ABOVE: Glasstech's automotive bending and tempering systems ensure consistent quality control to meet the strict size and shape tolerances required for encapsulation and flush glazing.

LEFT: The flat, high-optical quality glass tempered on Glasstech systems has been recognized by architects and designers as the preferred standard in the industry.

In Golden, Colorado, Glasstech Solar, Inc., is a leader in the development and commercialization of the many uses for thin-film, amorphous silicon. One of the most promising uses for this product is in photovoltaic cells to harness the sun's rays and transform them into electrical energy. Glasstech Solar has developed an efficient, proprietary technique and the equipment to coat glass panels with amorphous solicon.

Solar Cells, Inc., in Toledo, Ohio, was created to utilize Glasstech Solar's technology and ma-chines to coat and manufacture glass solar panels for use as automobile sun roofs and for the electric utility industry. Solar Cells has announced plans to build a multimillion-dollar solar power electrical generating field at a site within the Toledo Edison service area in northwestern Ohio.

Additionally, McMaster personally has funded ongoing research at The University of Toledo concerned with the development of a new concept in rotary engines for vehicular travel. The second part of this research is the develop-ment of a non-petroleum fuel source to power the rotary engine. Solar energy is used to process the fuel.

Glasstech, Inc., and Glasstech Limited, its sales and service subsidiary in Worcester, England, were sold to Naragansett Capital, Inc. (NCI), in Providence, Rhode Island. The NCI association provides Glasstech with the capital necessary to continue being the leader in the design and manufacture of glass bending and tempering systems used worldwide.

The future of Glasstech, Inc., is tied directly to the continuation of the innovative spirit that propelled the company from a second-floor office in Milbury, Ohio, to a company with worldwide involvement.

Libbey-Owens-Ford Co.

ABOVE: Libbey-Owens-Ford Co. is one of the world's largest manufacturers of automotive safety glass and other high-quality glass products.

LEFT: "All of our efforts spring from a central mission, which is to be the overall best supplier of glass in the world."

Libbey-Owens-Ford Co. is one of the world's largest manufacturers of automotive safety glass and is a major supplier of architectural, mirror, tinted, reflective-coated, and furniture glass products. For more than 60 years the company name has been synonymous with leadership, high quality, and innovative glass products.

The glassmaking industry in Toledo had its roots back in the late 1800s, when two men, Edward Drummond Libbey and Edward Ford, each decided to start businesses in the Toledo area. Ford founded the Edward Ford Plate Glass Company in Rossford, and Libbey joined together with an inventive genius, Michael J. Owens, to form the Libbey-Owens Sheet

GM's automotive windshields and windows.

LOF remained an independent corporation for 56 years until 1986, when the name and glass interests were acquired by the Pilkington Group. Headquartered in England, Pilkington is widely recognized as the worldwide technology leader in glassmaking. LOF status under this new leadership has become one of an autonomous operating company, with full access to the global resources of the Pilkington Group. In 1989 Nippon Sheet Glass, a joint venture partner with LOF for more than two decades, purchased 20 percent of Libbey-Owens-Ford.

Glass Company.

These two businesses operated separately until 1930, when they merged and created the Libbey-Owens-Ford Glass Company. The new company received a big boost one year later when it contracted with General Motors in nearby Detroit, Michigan, to be the exclusive supplier of all of

LOF credits much of its success through the years to the major emphasis it has placed on research and development efforts that have resulted in both new process technology and new glass products. Some of these have included Thermopane® insulating glass; Vari-Tran™ reflective glass; curved, wraparound, and shaded

windshields; Super Shock Absorber™ windshield; Antenna windshield; ElectriClear™ heated windshield systems; Safe-Ply™ anti-lacerative windshield; EZ-KOOL™ solar-control glass; and KOOLOF™ solar-coated glass.

"All of our efforts," says Dr. Ronald Skeddle, chief executive officer and president, "spring from a central mission, which is to be the overall best supplier of glass in the world. To us at LOF this starts with providing the absolute best customer service, enhanced by the on-time delivery of exceptional high-quality products."

LOF practices a participatory management style and operating philosophy that enables employees to play an active role in decision making. The company believes this team approach helps foster personal involvement and commitment and helps the entire LOF organization produce the best solutions to customer needs, time after time.

"The unique high quality of our products and services and the strength of the LOF organization

LOF's Flat Glass Products Group produces a variety of sophisticated glass products for the architectural and residential markets.

have been due to the quality and innovative spirit of our people," says Skeddle. "It has been this spirit of playing the game to win, backed by our commitment to work, our will to succeed, and our ability to learn, that has fueled and will continue to fuel our drive to develop, manufacture, and market the world's best glass products."

LOF's Original Equipment Automotive Products Group is a major supplier to the automotive industry. With fabrication facilities in the United States and Mexico, and joint ventures as close as Kentucky and as distant as South Korea, LOF maintains a true worldwide presence in automotive glass manufacturing.

Central to the development and production of high-quality, innovative automotive glass products is the idea of early involvement. LOF is a strong believer in concept-to-completion involvement. While new cars are still on the drawing board—or on a computer-aided design screen—LOF is there, assessing what the automakers' specific needs will be and working to meet those needs.

Today's design trends are influenced by the need for improved aerodynamics and are reflected by the move toward increased glass use for greater vision and safety in lighter, more fuel efficient vehicles. LOF has demonstrated its on-

going commitment to the auto industry by developing the facilities and resources necessary to meet these new design challenges.

Long after an auto leaves the showroom floor comes the need by the car-buying public for quality replacement parts. LOF's Automotive Glass Replacement Group meets those market needs with high-quality LOF replacement glass that is identical to original-equipment components. The LOF commitment to serve the automotive market from original concept, design, and delivery through quality replacement service remains a key strength.

LOF's Flat Glass Products Group produces a variety of sophisticated glass products for the architectural, residential, mirror, and furniture markets. This area of the company provides architects with superior glazing products that not only capitalize on emerging trends in design but help meet building performance criteria.

LOF products in the architectural market include not only clear and tinted glass, but also revolutionary products such as Eclipse™ reflective glass, a float glass with excellent solar control performance,

and Mirropane EP™, a transparent mirror for commercial and residential use.

It is the advanced state of LOF's on-line coating technology that is at the core of many of its new developments, including a new generation of thermal performance glass that is currently being manufactured for residential use. Along with these new high-technology products, LOF continues to manufacture its well-known Thermopane® insulating glass.

The overall quality demanded by the mirror and furniture industry is extremely rigid, and Libbey-Owens-Ford Co. plays a key role in supplying products that meet the needs of leading manufacturers. Precision manufacturing, attention to detail, and an insistence on perfection result in glass that consistently meets the exacting standards necessary for the creation of fine furniture and optically true mirrors.

Skeddle says, "Our winning attitude, our commitment to quality, and consistent improvement in the areas in which we do business are all constants that enable LOF to succeed in an increasingly competitive global marketplace."

The Kroger Company

1924 was a fascinating year for the Kroger Company and Toledo. The city's downtown was booming, and gangster activity was rampant. The *Toledo Blade* had been in business for 90 years, and grocery shopping in town changed forever with the arrival of the Kroger Grocery and Baking Company.

Barney Kroger's first move in Toledo was to buy the Tiedtke "Thrift Stores." Tiedtke's visionary thrift store concept involved supplementing its huge downtown store with smaller neighborhood markets. That location was later replaced with a larger store boasting 6,800 square feet of space. According to a front-page *Blade* report, "All Toledo hailed Kroger's modern approach to food shopping." The grand opening was attended by hundreds in the first few hours. Parents enjoyed the "marvelous self-serve grocery displays," and children received Shirley Temple pictures.

By 1957 Kroger made an unquestionable statement of dedication to Toledo with the opening of the former Swayne Field store. It was, at the time, the entire chain's largest and most modern store—and the first to install "space-age air doors." 1982 saw the com-

pany's largest single expansion, with 10 new stores opened or planned, creating nearly 1,000 new jobs (double the previous year's total). This was also the beginning of Kroger's role as a developmental anchor for small neighborhood shopping plazas. Kroger's vote of confidence attracted millions of investment dollars to Toledo and its suburbs. Today Kroger provides approximately 2,000 jobs.

The store of the 1990s is an amazing eight times the size of the 1924 model, averaging 55,000 to 60,000 square feet. And while the dedication to convenience and service is unchanged from Barney's days, it encompasses a great deal more.

Commitment to the highest-quality produce and meat and a large selection and variety of items in all categories is standard in any Kroger store. In addition, the bakery, deli, and fresh seafood departments enhance the one-stop-shopping concept. But today convenience and service mean providing a wide range of spe-

cialty departments which will save the most precious commodities: time. These departments include the Floral Shoppe; Kroger Catering; a salad and soup bar; video rentals; ready-to-cook, in-store chef-prepared Gourmet-to-Go entrees; and in-store banking facilities called Bank Marts.

While Kroger's presence in the community in terms of capital investment and jobs is impressive, and its contributions and innovations in the grocery industry are well-recognized, the company is most noted for its positive impact on the quality-of-life for Toledo-area residents. These efforts have been focused in several areas.

The Arts:
Kroger's goal is to provide exposure for arts organizations so that as many residents as possible can benefit from the performances and events offered. The Toledo Ballet Association credits Kroger for its recent notable achievements and growth in its corporate base; Kroger catering contributions allow Toledo Botanical Garden to host a Crosby Festival Preview fund-raiser, proceeds of which enable and fund year-round artist programs; and The Toledo Museum of Art enjoys support of its annual membership drive as well as ongoing family programs. In 1990 the Kroger Company was proud to receive the Arts Commission of Greater Toledo's Award for Community Support of the Arts.

Human Services:
During the 1989 United Way campaign, the Kroger Company employees achieved the highest rate of giving of any in the community, and during the 1990 campaign they increased that rate by

The Kroger Grocery and Baking Company arrived in Toledo in 1924.

five percent. This commitment to making a better place for those less fortunate is demonstrated not only through United Way, but through other fund-raising campaigns and events as well as the American Diabetes Association's Golf Tournament; the March of Dimes' WalkAmerica; the Easter Seals' Root Beer Float sale; and the United Health Services' Riboff In recognition of its many contributions to the community, Kroger received the first Outstanding Corporate Philanthropy award from The Greater Toledo Area Chapter of the National Society of Fund Raising Executives in 1990.

Community Events:
It has become commonplace for area residents to see Kroger banners at the majority of community events. This is often the most visible sign of Kroger's involvement but by no means the only one. Kroger's support and promotional aid enables organizations such as CitiFest and Toledo City-Parks to provide high-quality family events which serve the entire community: Eggstravaganza; Pumpkinarama; July 4th; and the Toledo Festival of the Arts. Larger, longer events such as the Jamie Farr LPGA Tournament provide positive national recognition for Toledo, and Kroger is pleased to be a major sponsor of these efforts as well.

Institutions:
Kroger's long-term commitment to Toledo's future is manifested through its capital commitment to several institutions. The company's participation in The Partnership Campaign—Education and the Arts (the joint campaign of the Toledo Museum of Art and The University of Toledo for the future construction of the Art Education Building) helps to ensure the growth and enrichment of two of Toledo's educational cornerstones. Further support of the University is provided by generous funding for the Athletic Department, and The Lyle Everingham Scholarship Fund in the College of Business, established in honor of the company's recently-retired chairman. A third institution which benefits from Kroger support is The Toledo Zoo, through contributions to building funds and the purchase of animals for new exhibits such as the penguins.

Life-Style Programs:
Recognizing that not everything good in the Toledo area happens at a place or event, Kroger is actively involved in promoting important long-term values which benefit individuals and the larger community. Healthy Choices, in conjunction with Toledo Hospital, focuses on elements which allow us to live longer, healthier lives: nutrition, preventive-measure screenings, information. Serving as recycling collection stations 52 weeks a year emphasizes the Kroger stores' commitment to serving as part of the solution to our growing environmental problems. And in an effort to foster financial responsibility in young people, Kroger has estab-

ABOVE LEFT: Today, Kroger stores meet consumers' multiple needs.

BELOW: The Kroger/CityParks Pumpkinarama is just one of the community events the Kroger Company sponsors and supports throughout the year.

lished, along with Fifth Third Bank, a KidSavers Club which will teach children the importance of saving for the future.

The Kroger Company embraces the philosophy that "doing good is good business." Following that thinking since 1924 has positioned the company as the market leader in Toledo, a position and partnership Kroger is committed to maintaining.

TL Industries, Inc.

Tuck Lee's coworkers at the radio station told him that if he wanted a degree in engineering he should enroll at Ohio State University or the University of Michigan. It sounds like simple advice, except that Tuck Lee was living in Korea at the time. But Lee was a man with a dream, and before long he found himself behind a desk in Ann Arbor as a student at the University of Michigan. He has come a long way since then. Today he operates a thriving microcomputer design and manufacturing firm that has sales in excess of $10 million annually. The company is headquartered in Northwood, Ohio, and employs more than 100 people.

"We offer the full range of services required to successfully design, implement, and produce reliable, cost-effective control systems," Lee says. Product development partnerships are one of the strengths of TL Industries—from the conceptual stage through prototype, testing, start-up production, and volume manufacturing, plus ongoing technical support services after the sale. "Quality, service, and competitive pricing are the three main criteria through which our customers measure our performance and our products," Lee says. "Quite simply, our philosophy is to provide the most technically advanced, cost-effective solutions to meet the diverse needs of our customers," he adds.

TL Industries was founded by Lee in the early 1970s. It was a perfect time to enter the exploding computer business, and Lee was among the first to apply the emerging microcomputer technology to solve industrial control problems.

TL Industries' manufacturing capabilities have grown as the

ABOVE: (Front left to right) Tuck B. Lee, president; Ham Hi Lee, vice president, treasurer. (Back left to right) Richard Blausey, vice president/engineering; Joseph Young, vice president/finance; Ted Stechschulte, vice president/manufacturing; David Clay, vice president/research and development.

RIGHT: The TL Industries' TVME-1611 VME Bus single board computer is used in many industrial control systems.

microcomputer industry has grown. Early products consisted of a few integrated circuits hand assembled on a small printed circuit board. The company now has the equipment and trained personnel for automatic placement and infrared reflow soldering of surface mount components. In fact, printed circuit boards with more than 100 integrated circuits are not uncommon.

Lee added a sheet-metal division recently to provide a reliable source of high-quality enclosures for the computer systems the company makes. The metal shop is now equipped with computer-controlled state-of-the-art equipment for cutting, punching, and forming sheet metal.

These days Lee is stepping back from the day-to-day operation of the business and devoting more time to developing new products for the company. "I've hired a top-quality team to run things," Lee says. He adds that he is also trying to spend more time with his family. "When you're building a business of your own the key ingredient for success is a supportive family," he says. "I wouldn't be where I am today if my wife hadn't been beside me every step of the way. It wasn't always easy, but she always made it seem like it was," he adds.

What does the future hold for TL Industries? Lee sees more growth. "We have traditionally expanded in two ways—by entering new industries and by adding new capabilities," Lee says. As technology in the microcomputer industry expands, TL Industries, Inc., will continue with these two growth avenues. In addition, it plans to pursue new growth by expanding the company's primary service area. Historically, most of its customers have been in the Toledo and Detroit areas. The bulk of new business has come from word-of-mouth advertising. The next level of growth Lee sees coming is through planned marketing and the use of a manufacturer's representative organization to cover a wider marketing territory.

Sun Oil Company

The oil business came to Toledo as a result of oil discoveries near Lima, Ohio, in 1885. The interest of Joseph Newton Pew and Edward Octavius Emerson, two oil entrepreneurs in Pennsylvania, was sparked, and early in the next year Joseph sent his nephew, Robert C. Pew, to investigate the new oil fields and the feasibility of securing leases. Robert's investigation led to the acquisition of two leases in Findlay Township for oil exploration, drilling, and production. The purchase of both leases on March 27, 1886, cost a total of $4,500 and was the beginning of the Sun Oil Company.

As oil production boomed in the state, Toledo rapidly became a refining and distribution center. Sun competed well with the larger and more established oil companies through the years, largely because it was a fully integrated company managing its own marketing organization, operating its own refineries, and controlling its own transportation network.

Another important factor in Sun's growth was its emphasis on innovation. Sun was one of the first to develop an anti-knocking gasoline and its Mercury-made motor oils. It was also the first to use the Houdry catalytic cracker to refine oil, which not only produced more gasoline but gasoline of high octane quality; and the company was the first to introduce a custom blending pump. Today the firm has the highest octane gasoline in a major brand, Ultra 94.

Sun has always been very supportive of employees' activities, especially through the Sun Employee Recreation Association. The company purchased 42 acres of property for use by employees and their families, and it is the site of Christmas parties, summer picnics, softball games, and swimming. The company feels it plays a vital role in the development of activities that draw employees and their families closer together.

Throughout the years Sun has also stressed the importance of corporate citizenship with its emphasis on local charities. Most notable are its support of United Way, matching 50 cents on every dollar that employees give; underwriting for Music Under The Stars, a free concert series for families; and funding for the establishment of the St. Vincent Medical Center Burn Unit. All scrap from the refinery is also donated to the St. Vincent Life Flight Helicopter.

The Toledo refinery is the oldest refinery in Sun Company and will be celebrating its 100th anniversary in 1994. The refinery is in the process of upgrading all its control rooms, making them more efficient and reliable. The Toledo facility employs more than 500 people.

Sun's Toledo refinery at night.

Photo by Brad Crooks

Patrons

The following individuals, companies, and organizations have made a valuable commitment to the quality of this publication. Windsor Publications gratefully acknowledges their participation in *Toledo: Focused for the Future.*

Columbia Gas of Ohio*
Consolidated Environmental Services, Inc.*
Dana Corporation*
Envirosafe Services, Inc.*
Fuller & Henry*

Glasstech, Inc.*
Hospital Council of Northwest Ohio*
Hydra-matic Division*
The Kroger Company*
Libbey-Owens-Ford Co.*
NFO Research, Inc.*
Owens-Corning Fiberglas*
The Schroeder Company*
Seaway Food Town*
Shumaker, Loop & Kendrick*
Software Alternatives, Inc.*
Spengler, Nathanson, Heyman, McCarthy & Durfee*

Sun Oil Company*
TL Industries, Inc.*
Toledo Hilton*
The Toledo Marriott*
The University of Toledo*
Watkins, Bates, Carey & McHugh*
WTVG-TV*

*Participants in Part Two, "Toledo's Enterprise's." The stories of these companies and organizations appear in chapters 6 through 10, beginning on page 86.

Selected Reading List

Downes, Randolph C. *The Conquest,* Vol. I, *Canal Days,* Vol. II, Lucas County Historical Series. Toledo: Maumee Valley Historical Society, 1968.

————. *Lake Port,* Vol. III, Lucas County Historical Series. Toledo: The Historical Society of Northwestern Ohio, 1951.

————. *Industrial Beginnings,* Vol IV, Lucas County Historical Series. Toledo: The Historical Society of Northwestern Ohio, 1954.

Doyle, John H. *A Story of Early Toledo.* Bowling Green, Ohio: C.S. Van Tassel, Managing Publisher, 1919.

Edwards, Richard. *Toledo— Historical and Descriptive.* Toledo: Toledo Commercial Company, 1876.

Glaab, Charles N., and Morgan J. Barclay. *Toledo: Gateway to the Great Lakes.* Tulsa, Oklahoma: Continental Heritage Press, 1982.

Harrison, John M. *The Blade of Toledo.* Toledo: Toledo Blade Co., 1985.

Illman, Harry R. *Unholy Toledo.* San Francisco: Polemic Press Publications, Inc., 1985.

Killits, John M., A.M., LL.D., ed. *Toledo and Lucas County, Ohio 1623-1923,* Volumes I, II, and III. Chicago and Toledo: The S.J. Clarke Publishing Company, 1923.

Knapp, H.S. *History of the Maumee Valley.* Toledo: n.p., 1877.

Porter, Tana Mosier. *Toledo Profile: A Sesquicentennial History.* Toledo: Toledo Sesquicentennial Commission, 1987.

Root, Randall. *Toledo Toward 2000.* Toledo: The Port Lawrence Company, 1983.

Scribner, Harvey, ed. *Memoirs of Lucas County and the City of Toledo,* Vol. I and II. Madison, Wis.: Western Historical Association, 1910.

Slocum, Charles Elihu, M.D., Ph.D., LL.D. *History of the Maumee River Basin.* Defiance, Ohio: Charles Elihu Slocum, 1905.

Staelin, Carl G. *Toledo Highlights.* Toledo: The Rotary Club of Toledo, Ohio, 1966.

Toledo Metropolitan Cityguide, Vol. II. Toledo: Lawrence Publications, Inc., 1988.

Van Voorhis Wendler, Marilyn. *The Foot of the Rapids: The Biography of a River Town—Maumee, OH—1988.* Canton, Ohio: Daring Books, 1988.

Waggoner, Clark, ed. *History of the City of Toledo and Lucas County, Ohio.* New York and Toledo: Munsell & Company, Publishers, 1888.

Wright, Isaac. *The East Side—Past and Present.* Toledo: The Second Congregational Church, 1894.

Directory of Corporate Sponsors

Columbia Gas of Ohio, 88
701 Jefferson Avenue
Toledo, OH 43653
419-248-5188
L. Craig Bergman

Consolidated Environmental Services, Inc., 113
26372 Glenwood Road
Perrysburg, OH 43551
419-874-0782
Dennis A. Siefke

Dana Corporation, 124-125
4500 Dorr
Post Office Box 1000
Toledo, OH 43697
419-535-4520
Thomas J. Fairhurst

Envirosafe Services, Inc., 112
1600 Madison Avenue
Toledo, OH 43624
419-255-5100
Jack A. Murphy

Fuller & Henry, 95
One Seagate
Toledo, OH 43603
419-247-2500
Donald Hawkins

Glasstech, Inc., 128-129
Ampoint Ind. Complex
995 4th Street
Perrysburg, OH 43551
419-661-9500

Hospital Council of Northwest Ohio, 108-111
5515 Southwyck Boulevard, #203
Toledo, OH 43614
419-865-1275
W. Scott Fry

Hydra-matic Division, 127
1455 West Alexis Road
Toledo, OH 43612
419-470-5192
Jeffrey S. Kuhlman

The Kroger Company, 132-133
4533 Monroe Street
Toledo, OH 43613
614-898-3235
Dale Hollandsworth

Libbey-Owens-Ford Co., 130-131
811 Madison Avenue
Toledo, OH 43695-0799
419-247-4773
C. Craig Washing

NFO Research, Inc., 100-101
2700 Oregon Road
Northwood, OH 43619
419-666-8800
Ron Swift

Owens-Corning Fiberglas, 126
Fiberglas Tower
Toledo, OH 43659
419-248-8220
Brad Oelman

The Schroeder Company, 102
4668 Talmadge Road
Post Office Box 8890
Toledo, OH 43623
419-473-0473
Kay Silvis

Seaway Food Town, 118-119
1020 Ford Street
Maumee, OH 43537
419-893-9401
Richard B. Iott

Shumaker, Loop & Kendrick, 92-93
1000 Jackson
Toledo, OH 43624
419-241-9000
Donald M. Mewhort, Jr.

Software Alternatives, Inc., 96-97
1684 Woodlands Drive
Arrowhead Park
Maumee, OH 43537
419-891-7200
Michael J. Delverne

Spengler, Nathanson, Heyman, McCarthy & Durfee, 98-99
1000 National Bank Building
Toledo, OH 43604
419-241-2201
Pat Krajovic

Sun Oil Company, 135
1819 Woodville
Oregon, OH 43616
419-698-6624
Valorie J.H. Juergens

TL Industries, Inc., 134
2541 Tracy Road
Northwood, OH 43619
419-666-8144
Tuck B. Lee

Toledo Hilton, 120
3100 Glendale Avenue
Toledo, OH 43614
419-381-6800
Fred Reese

The Toledo Marriott, 116-117
#2 Seagate, Summit Street
Toledo, OH 43604
419-241-1411
Nancy Cimney

The University of Toledo, 106-107
2801 West Bancroft Street
Toledo, OH 43606
419-537-2675
Fred Mollenkopf

Watkins, Bates, Carey & McHugh, 94
National Bank Building
Toledo, OH 43604
419-241-2100
William F. Bates

WTVG-TV, 89
4247 Dorr Street
Toledo, OH 42607
419-531-1313
James M. Nowak

Index

Italicized numbers indicate illustrations.

A

A.A. Pope American Bicycle Company, 11
Actors Equity Association, 59
African Savanna, 65
Agriculture, 15
Air freight, 45-47
American Academy of Ophthalmology, 69
American Political Science Association, 51
Ampoint Industrial Complex, 36
Amtrak terminal, *44*
Andersons, The, 29
AP Parts, 28
Arrowhead Park, 21, 35-36
Arts, 24, 52, 54, 56-59
Asian community, 72, 81
Automotive Corridor, 47
Automotive industry, 11, 29, 32

B

Bailey, Dean 37, 38
Baseball, 67
Bassett family, 59
Beaugrande, John Baptiste, 10
Bedford Township, 20
Beirut Restaurant & Lounge, 81
Bell, Michael P., *75*
Bicycle manufacturing, 11
Bird House, 65
Birmingham, 77
Black community, 72, 74-75
Blade, The, 14, 28, 49, 51, 58, 74, 81
Blade Run, 77
Blue Stockings, 67
Bluffton College, 63
Board of Community Relations, 75
Boating, 15, *15,* 22-23, 24, 68
Bollinger, Marie, 57
Bostwick-Braun Company, 28
Bowling, 24, 67
Bowling Green State University, 30, 32, 41, 60-61, *61,* 82
Bowling Hall of Fame, 67
BP Oil Company, 29
Brower, William, 74
Brownlee, Alexander, 72
Bulgarian Cultural Society, 77
Bulgarian/Macedonian community, 76-77

Bulgarian Macedonian Cultural Center, 76-77
Burlington Air Express, 41, 45-46, 47, 51
Byblos Restaurant, 82

C

Cake-walkin' Jass Band, 83
Canals, 10, 42, 78
Cargill grain terminal, 30
Carter, Jimmy, 83
Casa Di Maria Restaurant, 82
Cassatt, Mary, 69
Cedar Business Center, 36
Centennial Hall, 17
Centennial Mall, 60
Central Catholic High School, 25
CentreStage Productions, Ltd., *57,* 59
Champion Spark Plug Company, 29, 32, 74
Chrysler Jeep plant, 11, 29, *33*
Cinco de Mayo, 76
City/County Building, 17
Civil War, 44, 74
Cleveland Orchestra, 56
Collingwood Arts Center, 59
Commodore Perry, 42
Compaan, Alvin, 32
Conrail, 45
Cook, Gene, 67
Crosby Gardens, 75
CSX railroad, 44, 45, *45*

D

Dana Corporation, 29
Dance, 56, 57
Davis Business College, 63
Day, Bill, 36
Defiance College, 63
Degas, Edgar, 69
De Leon, Margarita, 75, 76
Denver, John, 16-17, 68
Detroit Metro Airport, 47
Detroit Symphony, 56
Detroit Tigers, 67
DeVilbiss, Allen, 11
DeVilbiss Company, 11
DeVilbiss, Jr., Allen, 11
DeVilbiss, Thomas, 11
Diamond Club, 67
Dieciseis de Septiembre, 76
Digital Equipment Corporation, 32
Doehler-Jarvis, 29

Downtown, 16, 17, 19, 28-29
Doyle, Sir Arthur Conan, 69
Dura Automatic Hardware, 29

E

East Toledo, 20
Economic development, 29-30, 40
Edison Industrial Systems Center, 32
Education, 22, 24, 30, 32, 59-61, 63
Edward Ford Plate Glass Company, 11
Eisenhower, Dwight D., 11
El Grupo Cultural Latinoamericano, 76
Elmore, 21
Emmick, Vincent J., 72
Empire Theater, 81
Employment, 22, 28, 29, 32-33, 36, 46, 72
English community, 72, 74
Ercegan, Milan, 68
Erie and Kalamazoo railroad, 42
Erie Canal, 78
Erie Islands, 68
Ethnic communities, 70, 72-81, 82
Exmoor, 20
Eye Center of Toledo, 69

F

Fallen Timbers State Memorial and Monument, 65
Farr, Jamie, 79, 81, 83
Festival of the Arts, 64, 75
Fiberglass industry, 26-27, 28
Fiberglas Tower, 28, *30*
Fifth Third Bank, 29
Finch, Robert, 72
Findlay College, 63
Fishing, 15, 24, 68
Flournoy & Gibbs, 41
Folk Festival, 64
Ford, Edward, 11
Ford Motor Company, 29
Foreign trade zone, 46
Fort Industry Square, 35
Fort Meigs, *11*
Four SeaGate, 35
Fourth of July, 72-73
Franciscan Life Center, 56, 57, 58
Franklin Park Mall, 36-37, *40*
Freighters, 45, 49
French community, 72
Frogtown, 10, 19

G

Galvin, Kent J., 22
Gearhart, Tom, 58
Gendron, Peter, 11, 74
General Mills, Inc., 29
General Motors, 29
Genoa, 21
Geography, 15
German-American Festival, 78
German community, 72, 74, 78
Glaab, Charles N., 42
Glass Bowl, 67
Glass Bowl Stadium, 60
Glass City Autosport, 26
Glass City Gymnastics, 26
Glass City Roofing, 26
Glass industry, 10, 26, 28
Glassline Corporation, 28
Glass-related industry, 28
Glasstech, Inc., 28, 29, 32
Godfrey, Gabriel, 10
Golf, 24
Government, 17, 25
Great Black Swamp, 65
Great Eastern mall, 37
Great Lakes freighters, 45, 49
Greek-American Festival, 78, *80-81*
Greek community, 76, 78
Guys & Dolls, 56-57, *57*

H

Hadzi, Dimitri, 33, 35
Harrison, William Henry, 11
Harvey, Hank, 14, 49, 51, *51*
Hasty Hills, 20, *21*
Havens, Jim, *58*
Heidelberg College, 63
Hewlett-Packard Corporation, 32
Highland Meadows Golf Club, 24
High-tech industry, 30, 32
Highway Handbook, 51
Hillsdale College, 63
Hispanic community, 72, 74, 75-76
Holland Township, 20-21
Holy Trinity Greek Orthodox
    Church, 78
Honda, 32
Horvath, Nancy Packo, 83, *83*
Horvath, Robin, 83
Hungarian community, 72, 73, 76,
    77-78, 83

I

IMAGE, 76

Immigrants, 10
Imperial Lanes, 67
Industrial parks, 33, 35-36
Industry, 26, 28-30, 32-33
Intermodal shipping, 49
International Amateur Wrestling
    Federation, 68
International Institute of Greater
    Toledo, 70, 81
International Park, 12, 70, 72
Interstate 75, 47
Interstate Lanes, 67
Inverness Country Club, 24
Irish community, 72, 74
Irish Hills, 15, 16

J

JAMA, 69
Jeeps, 11, 29, 33
Jerome Library, 61
Jewish community, 78
Jewish Community Center, *79*
Jewish Federation of Greater
    Toledo, 78
Jing Chuan, 82
John F. Savage Hall, 68
Johns-Manville, 26
Jones, Samuel M. "Golden Rule," 72

K

Kid's Fishing Rodeo, 4
Kraus, William, 72, 78

L

LaGrange Street, 73, 74
LaGrange Street Festival, 74
Lake Erie, 15, 24, 42, 44, 68
Lambertville, 15, 20
Lasalle, Jacob, 78
Lasalle & Koch, 78-79
La Traviata, 57, *57*
Lawrence Publications, 19
Lebanese community, 79, 81
Lenk, Peter, 78
Libbey, Edward Drummond, 10-11,
    19, 54, 56, 74
Libbey, Florence, 56
Libbey Glass Company, 10
Libbey-Owens-Ford Glass
    Company, 11, 26, 28, *28*, 29, 32,
    82
Libbey-Owens Sheet Glass Com-
    pany, 11
Lima Citizen, 51

LOF Tower, 28
Lourdes College, 56, 57, 58, 63
Lozier Manufacturing Company,
    11
LPGA Jamie Farr Toledo Open, 24
Lucas, Robert, 10
Lucas County Courthouse, 17, *17*,
    19
Lucas County Recreation Center,
    67, *67*

M

Macedonian/Bulgarian community,
    76-77
McHugh, Connie, 25
McHugh, John, 25, *25*
McKinley, William, 17, 19
McMaster Hall, 60
Magyar Reformed Church, 73
Manor House, 65
Manos Greek Restaurant & Up-
    stairs Bar & Grill, 82, *82*
Manufacturing, 22, 29, 30
Manville Sales Corporation, 26, 28
Mariott Hotel, 35
Marx, Emil, 78
Marx, Guido, 72, 78
Marx, Joseph, 78
Masonic Auditorium, 56, 57
Mass transit, 50
Maumee, 10, 20, 21
Maumee Bay, 15
Maumee Bay State Park, 24, 65, *66*
Maumee River, *2-3*, 10, *12-13*, *14*,
    15, 20, 21, 42, 70
Maumee Valley Day School, 59
Mazda, 32
Media, 28
Medical College of Ohio, 32, 59-60,
    69
Meena, James, 57
Metcalf Field, 47
Metroparks, 64, *64*, 65
Michigan Southern railroad, 42
Millbury, 21
Miller, Carlaine, 58
Mills, Norb, 58, 59
Ming's Dynasty, 82
Miracle Mile mall, 37
Missouri Pacific Railroad, 51
Monet, Claude, 69
Monroe Street, 16, 17
Mosque, 81, *82*
Music, 56-57

N

NAACP, 74
National Business Hall of Fame, 35
National Institutes of Health, 69
National Malleable Castings Company, 72-73
National Open Tournaments, 24
Natural gas industry, 10
Neighborhoods, 16, 19-21, 24
New England Glass Company, 10
Nissan, 32
Norfolk-Southern railroad, 45
North Coast, 68
North Toledo, 19-20
North Towne Commons, 37
North Towne Square, 37, *40*
Northwest Ohio Bond Fund, 29-30
Northwest Ohio Hispanic Business Association, 76
Northwest Ohio Junior Achievement Business Hall of Fame, 35
Northwest Ohio Rib-Off, *73*
Northwest Territory Ordinance, 10
Northwood, 21

O

Oak Openings Center for Industry, 36
Oak Openings Preserve, 65, *65*
Ohio Associated Press, 51
Ohio Industrial Training Program, 24
Ohio Northern University, 63
Ohio State University, 15
Old West End, 16, *18*, 19, 54, 59
One Government Center, 17, *17*, 19
One SeaGate, 17, 33, *34-35*, 35, 36
Oregon, 21
Ottawa Hills, 16, 20, 21, 24
Ottawa Park, *4-5*
Owens-Corning Fiberglas, 26, 28, 30
Owens-Illinois, 26, 28, 30, 33, 36
Owens, Michael J., 10-11, 19, 61, 63, 74
Owens Technical College, 30, 41, *60*, 63

P

Packo, Jr., Tony, 83
Packo, Rose, 83
Packo, Tony, 83
Pappas, Pando, 76-77
Parks, 24, 65
Pawlicki, Clarence, D., 29
Pearson Metropark, 65
Performing arts, 56-59
Peristyle, The, 56
Perrysburg, 21
PGA Tournament, 24
Pilkington, 26
Plastics industry, 30
Point Place, 37
Polish community, 72, 73-74
Polish Day Annual Picnic, 74
Polymer Institute, 61
Pope Motor Car Company, 11
Population, 10, 21-22, 24, 25, 40, 44, 72, 73, 74, 75, 78
Port Alexis Industrial park, 36
Port Clinton, 68
Porter, J. Michael, 14
Porter, Tania Mosier, 19, 72, 73, 74, 77
Port Lawrence, 10, 16
Port of Toledo, 42, 44-45, *48*, 49, *49*
Portside festival marketplace, 35
Powell, Mary Alice, 81
Presley, Elvis, 51
Professional Bowlers Tour, 67
Promenade Park, *33*, 73

Q

Quilter, Barney, 65

R

Railroads, 14, 42, 44, 45, 49
R.A. Stranahan Arboretum, *8-9*
Ravin, Jim, 69, *69*
Ravin, Nancy, 69
Recreation, 52, 65, 67-68
Reptile House, 65
Restaurants, 81-82, 83
Retail industry, 36-37, 40
Reynolds, Burt, 83
Riverside Hospital, 75
Roadways, 14, 49-50
Romeis, Jacob, 72
Root, Deborah, 41
Root Publishing, 41
Root, Randall, 41, *41*
Rosary Cathedral, 19, *19*
Rossford, 11, 21
Roulet, Lloyd, 75
Royal Tool Inc., 28

S

St. Anthony's, 73
St. Hedwig's Catholic Church, 73
St. Lawrence Seaway, 11, 35, 49
St. Stephen's Hungarian Catholic Church, 73
St. Vincent Medical Center, 69
Sakura Gardens, 81
Saturday Night in Toledo, 16-17, 68
Scalzo, Jr., Joseph R., 68
Scalzo, Sr., Joseph R., 67-68
Scheets, George, 72
Schreiber, Cornell, 78
Schulte, Edward J., 12, 30
SeaGate Centre, 35, *37*
Seaway Foodtown, Inc., 29
Serchuk, Stephen W., 40
Shipping, 14, 35, 44-45, 46-47, 49-50
Shopping mall development, 36-37, 40
Side Cut Park, 65
Siena Heights College, 63
Simmons, Jr., J.B., 74-75
Skeldon, Ned, 67
Society Bank, 28-29, 67
Solar Cells, Inc., 30, 32
South Toledo, 20
Southwyck Lanes, 67
Southwyck Mall, 37, *38-39*
Sparks, Randy, 16
Spielbusch, Henry, 74
Sports, 24, 67-68
Springfield Meadows, 21
Springfield Township, 20-21
Spring Meadows mall, 37
SSOE, Inc., 29
Stautzenberger College, 63
Steamboats, 42
Stengel, Casey, 67
Stranahan, Duane, 74
Stranahan family, 65
Stranahan Hall, 60
Suburban Airport, 47
Suburban neighborhoods, 20-21
Summit Center, 35
Sun Oil Company, 67
Sun Refining, 29
Swan Creek Preserve, *52-53*
Swayne Field, 67
Sylvania, 16, 20, *21*
Sylvania Township, 20
Szyperski, Leonard, 73

T

Teledyne CAE, 29, 30
Temperance, 15, 20
Tempglass, Inc., 28
Thai Guy, 82
Theater, 57-59
Theos Taverna & Greek Restaurant, 82
Thin Film Institute, 32
Thomas, Danny, 79, 81
Thomas Edison Program, 32
Three SeaGate, 35
Tiffin University, 63
Toledo Area Chamber of Commerce, 14, 22
Toledo Area Governmental Research Association (TAGRA), 64
Toledo Area Regional Transit Authority (TARTA), 50
Toledo Ballet Association, 56
Toledo Ballet Company, 56, 57
Toledo Botanical Garden, *64*
Toledo Catholic diocese, 19
Toledo City Council, 67
Toledo Edison, 28
Toledo Express Airport, 11, 14, 45-47, *47*
ToldeoFest, *78, 79*
Toledo International Regatta, *76*
Toledo-Lucas County Port Authority, 12, 28, 29-30, 36, 41, 46, 49, 51
Toledo Masonic Auditorium, 56, 57
Toledo Metropolitan Cityguide, 19
Toledo Metropolitan Statistical Area, 21-22, 24
Toledo Mud Hens, 24, 67, *67*

Toledo Museum of Art, 19, 24, 52, 54, *54, 55*, 56
Toledo Opera Company, 24, 56-57, *57*
"Toledo Profile," 72
Toledo Repertoire Theatre, 57, 58-59
Toledo Scale and Cash Register Company, 11
Toledo Sesquicentennial Commission, 72
Toledo Symphony Orchestra, 24, 56, *58*
Toledo War, 10
Toledo Zoo, 24, *62-63*, 63-65
Toledo Zoological Society, 64
Tony Packo Food Company, 83
Tony Packo's Cafe, 81, 83
Toyota, 32
Transportation industry, 44-47, 49-50, 51
Trinity Church, 35
TRINOVA Corporation, 29
Triple-A Alliance of Professional Baseball, 67
Trucking industry, 14, 45, 46, 47, 49, *50*

U

Ujvagi, Peter, 77-78
Underground Railroad, 74
United Parcel Service, 41
University Hall, 60
University of Michigan, 15, 30, 51, 69
University of Toledo, 9, 17, 25, 30, 32, 41, 42, 58, *59*, 60, 61,

61, 68, 82
USA Weekend magazine, 65
UT Community Technical College, 30
UT Polymer Institute, 30

V

Ventura's, 82
Village Players, 57, 58-59
Vistula, 10, 16
Visual arts, 52, 54, 56

W

Walden Pond, *4-5*
Walker, Moses Fleetwood, 67
Watson, Donna Petcoff, 77
Western Basin, 68
Western Lake Erie, 68
Westgate Dinner Theatre, 57, 59
Westgate Mall, 36-37, 59
West Toledo, 19-20, 24
WGTE-TV, 28
Wildwood Preserve, 65
Williams, Lee, 74
Willis B. Boyer, *12-13*
Willis Day Business Center, 36
Willys-Overland Company, 11
WNWO-TV, 28
Woodville Mall, 37
World Cup amateur wrestling, 67-68
Wrestling, 67-68
WTOL-TV, 28
WTVG-TV, 28

Y

Yamasaki, Minoru, 17